HEALING

from

WITHIN

BOOKS
IRH PRESS
New York

Library of Congress Cataloging-in-Publication Data

ISBN 13: 978-1-942125-18-1
ISBN 10: 1-942125-18-6

Printed in Canada
First Edition

Book Design: Karla Baker
Cover Images: © artnovielysa, © Mr.Vander / Fotolia
Interior Images: © seamni_sun, © Makkuro_GL, © oksanaok, © HN Works,
© teirin, © rashadashurov, © irina, © davooda, © teracreonte,
© mrswilkins, © atthameeni, © kusuriuri / Fotolia

HEALING
from
WITHIN

LIFE-CHANGING KEYS TO CALM, SPIRITUAL, AND HEALTHY LIVING

RYUHO OKAWA

AUTHOR OF 100 MILLION BOOKS SOLD WORLDWIDE

IRH PRESS

CONTENTS

Part II
Answering Questions on Healing from Within

CHAPTER 4

TREATMENTS FOR DISEASES AND DISORDERS

CHAPTER 5

MINDSETS FOR CAREGIVERS AND HEALTHCARE PROFESSIONALS

Part III
Healing Yourself with the Power of Faith

Prologue

YOUR MIND AND BODY

No one ever wants to come down with an illness.
But if that's the case,
Why are the major hospitals always
As crowded and busy as supermarkets?
We may think that we don't want to get sick
On the surface level of our consciousness.
But we are actually seeking illness
From the subconscious level of our mind.

You are subconsciously seeking illness
When you're facing a setback at work,
When you're feeling exhausted from constant schoolwork,
When you've been admonished,
When you feel humiliated and stripped of your pride,
When you need some time off
But can't get yourself to ask for it,
When you feel self-conscious about
Your inadequacies or limitations,
When you've become convinced that you're a hopeless failure,
When you're about to be crushed under
The weight of other people's expectations,
When you have no outlet for pent-up stress,
When negative thoughts feel convincing,
When you can't seem to restore a healthy rhythm

To your day-to-day life,
When you feel paralyzed by guilt.

By now, you have probably guessed what this all means:
Illness arises from a weakened heart and mind.
To heal our illness, then, we must pray, believe,
And eagerly seek to restore our inner strength.
For when we have a clear inner desire to heal,
Our body will respond.

Believe that your true nature is strong and healthy.
For your body's power to naturally heal
Will be fortified by
Your sense of hope,
Your determination,
And the power of the spiritual Truths.

—Ryuho Okawa, May 2008

Part **I**

Nurturing a Healthy
Mind-Body Connection

CHAPTER 1

ESSENTIAL DAILY PRACTICES FOR MENTAL AND PHYSICAL WELL-BEING

SPIRITUAL LIVING IS THE KEY TO YOUR HEALTH AND HEALING

Understanding Your Mind-Body Connection

Of all the physical possessions we cherish in this world, our health is perhaps the most precious: no amount of wealth can truly replace the sense of well-being that maintaining our health can bring to our lives. Being in good health lets us enjoy our lives to the fullest without depending on others for care and becoming a burden on them down the road. There's no doubt about the vital role that health plays in enhancing the longevity of our happiness as we live in this world.

Illness most often arises when we mentally or physically push beyond our limits in an effort to accomplish more than we can take on. Our health becomes prone to decline when we deprive our bodies of the care they need. And carelessness is bound to lead to frequent injuries. These are common mistakes made by people who believe strongly in "being tough" and are prone to depending on mental toughness and sheer grit—even at the expense of their physical well-being—to carry them through life's challenges.

But, if we hope to savor our happiness well into the evening of our life, it's best not to go on underestimating the value of our health. It's true that we exist in the other world only as spiritual intelligence. But here in this world, the body and the soul both make up who we are and work together through spiritual principles that allow them to act in unity. So when some kind of trouble afflicts our mind inwardly, it also manifests outwardly somewhere in the body. Likewise, when something within the body breaks down, the mind also begins to founder and deteriorate. Our mind and body are inextricably connected.

In modern times, more and more people are dying from cancer. In many cases, the reason our bodies are creating cancer is the wealth of mental stresses we have to handle in our lives today. This means that many people are literally dying from causes that arise from within the mind: the abundance of worries and distresses that are now rife in advanced societies. Since human beings were all born to materialize what we hold within our minds, the strain on our state of mind acts as a constant stream that directly influences the physical condition of our bodies. This inseparable union between the mind and body is why the turmoil we feel inwardly becomes mirrored externally in the form of diseases such as cancer.

 This does not by any means imply that cancer happens because we are bad people. But we all live under the daily pressures of modern-day stresses and are often unable to resiliently cope with them. The constant strain we experience may develop into a serious illness unless we are careful to take note when mental exhaustion and pervasive fear, anxiety, and angst are leading to the gradual ruin of our mind and body.

Your Mind and Body Are Always Affecting Each Other

There are many other common cases when our body is influenced by the wearing away of our mind. It is not uncommon to hear that a business owner who has been struggling through a bankruptcy or a huge financial crisis has broken down into illness. This is a clear case in which the mind collapsed under the heavy strain first and the physical condition followed, mirroring the mental deterioration with a physical illness.

The reverse of this process occurs when a physical disease leads us to accumulate mental strain and wears down our spirits until we are unable to hold back from spilling our discontents and dissatisfactions. We may even lash out at others and treat them harshly, spiraling into actions that breed disharmony with those around us. This is how a diseased body can gradually disease the mind, too. Buddhism has long taught that the mind and body work as one and has enlightened many to see them as an inseparable, unified whole, rather than as independent entities. This is because understanding how they work together helps us pay close attention to our overall health and notice when we need to give our body more attention and better care.

Gaining a better awareness of this relationship between the mind and body is the key to health and happiness. The secret to a healthy mind and body is finding the proper balance of nutrition, exercise, and rest. Balancing nutritious foods, good exercise, and restorative sleep is essential for our bodies to continuously produce energy and vitality. When something goes awry with our physical condition, it means that something has gone askew with one of these three foundations of health, and they are our body's signals telling us that they need to be restored to proper balance.

AWAKENING TO THE ONENESS OF YOUR MIND AND BODY

Your Mindset Determines Your Physical and Intellectual Development

As we have learned through discoveries in human biology, when human life is conceived within the womb, it follows a hereditary blueprint that gets passed down from our parents. But from the moment we are born into this world, our physiological development no longer follows just the prearranged path of our genetic makeup. Our development is also determined by the conscious choices we make to manage our health and well-being throughout life. In fact, these choices determine more than half of our physiological development.

For example, a child born to athletic parents may be blessed with an aptitude for athleticism. But this biological potentiality by itself can only go so far in contributing to the child's actual development into an athlete. The child's own decision to maintain a fit and active lifestyle is also essential for achieving that goal.

It is the same with other facets of human development, such as a child's aptitude for intelligence. While a child may be born into an intellectual family, her genes alone have limited influence on her mental development and need to be accompanied by conscious choices to nurture and educate her own mind.

Your Mind-Body Connection Is the Key to Your Health and Happiness

The mind and body work in constant union like a driver works in union with a car. Just as the driver controls the path of the car, the mind determines the course of the growth and well-being of our bodies.

Even precisely identical vehicles will handle very differently depending on who is behind the wheel. A driver with superior skill and a deep knowledge of the car's unique performance features will know how to drive it with grace, even through difficult road conditions. In contrast, the awkward skills of a novice taking the same vehicle—or even a better one—for a ride cannot be masked, no matter how superior the features of the car. And it is just as true that a vehicle of lower grade can offer a superb riding experience in the hands of an excellent driver—a much better ride, in fact, than even the highest-rated car in the hands of a bad driver.

Moreover, the attitude with which we operate and maintain our vehicle can shorten or extend the vehicle's lifespan and change how often it needs to go to the shop. The same holds true for the human body; the mindset we bring to how we care for our bodies determines the diseases we invite and our longevity.

So, we need not begin with strong and healthy genes to live a healthy, fit, disease-free life. Even if we begin life with a faulty vehicle, with regular maintenance and inspection, we can minimize the repairs that it will need. No matter what kind of body we were blessed with in this life, even one with a weak constitution, we can achieve a disease-free, healthful life by giving it proper care.

AN INVESTMENT IN YOUR HEALTH IS AN INVESTMENT IN LONGEVITY

The Money We Spend on Health Is an Essential Investment

There are basic measures you can take to manage and improve your health and well-being no matter what condition your health is in now. The first measure may come as a surprise if you have a religious aptitude or are expecting me to begin with spiritual advice specifically about the mind. The first and foremost advice I want to offer is quite the opposite of that: I recommend dedicating a portion of your wealth to your health. Doing so is so essential that I feel that it's hard to stress this enough. This requires a strong commitment and firm resolve to be unhesitating about spending money on your health. Our health is not the ideal place to practice financial restraint because, in the long term, we will pay the price for any stinginess we practice in the present.

The money we put toward our health should be considered an essential investment in our future, a necessary ongoing expense. It serves us best to think of it as the coal that we continuously feed into the engine to operate a train. Investing in our health financially allows us to consistently fuel our body so it can run smoothly throughout our journey. In this view, the practice of spending money on our health is good and heavenly in nature, and by no means something to feel guilty or shameful about. Have you been in the habit of using a part of your earnings each month to promote your physical well-being?

Those whose health is especially at risk are those who follow the unhealthy structure of urban lifestyles, rising early to beat the traffic and then not coming home until well into the night after having drinks and leaving no time for exercise. Everyone knows that this is a formula for weight gain.

Stop and consider for a moment, and notice that you feel no hesitation about spending money on alcohol and socializing. And then consider how much money you have applied toward exercise. This is a blind spot for most people. Most everyone has thought about how much or how little exercise they've done. But few, if any, have given thought to how much money they have spent on exercise.

Rather than being concerned with how many hours you should be putting into exercise, think of how much money you want to invest in ensuring that you'll get in the exercise you need. Shifting your perspective this way may open up new possibilities for managing your health that meet your specific lifestyle needs.

For example, let's say that your current monthly income is about $3,000. Just 10 percent of this income—$300—I would say, is a reasonable amount to dedicate to your health management needs. By setting aside these several hundred dollars, you create many possible options for yourself. With several hundred dollars, you can easily afford a membership at a gym or country club, swimming lessons, or cardio classes. Of course there are more economical forms of exercise, such as walking, jogging, and jump-roping. But, while these offer the best health benefits, they tend to be less pleasurable than other forms of exercise, which hampers motivation and sustainability. So I still recommend choosing other methods of getting exercise if your monthly earnings allow room for you to do so.

If your finances have room to breathe, it will serve you well in the long run to invest this money in your long-term health. On the other hand, if you have a job that requires a lot of physical exertion and you stay fit that way, it may be more beneficial to allow your body to rest and relax or treat yourself to a fancy dinner every once in a while.

If You Can't Invest Wealth, Then Invest Time

But what should you do if, even after considering setting aside part of your income for health management, you are unable to find the means to pay for the expenses? This brings us to the second measure for managing long-term health: instead of spending money, spend additional time. This is a chief principle. Getting up thirty minutes earlier to spend time on exercise is one common way to invest time in your health. You may also use a part of your Saturday and Sunday every week to devote yourself fully to exercise.

Many activities are either free or very inexpensive. In principle, walking is the place to begin. But many exercises, such as jump-roping, batting, practicing golf swings, and many others, incorporate equipment but in an economical way.

Last but not least, I would also like to mention the benefits of exercising with peers. Exercising with friends doesn't require any money at all but offers the advantage of moral support, which can be a necessity when it comes to sustaining a low-cost, active lifestyle throughout our lives. While we may feel apt to give up when we are all alone, exercising with a friend helps keep us motivated to persist in meeting our health goals.

WALKING: THE BASIS OF CARING FOR YOUR MIND AND BODY

Measuring Your Steps Daily

Even when we know that exercise is essential to our health and longevity, some of us still find the task of acclimating to a health-conscious lifestyle to be a great struggle. The struggle needn't be so daunting, however. There is a form of exercise that will allow you to ease into an active lifestyle. This method is walking.

Walking is no doubt the most basic form of human exercise, but it is one that can be relied on to benefit not only the body, but also the mind. In principle, a proper amount of walking is enough exercise to foster an active mind.

The main challenge, particularly for those who live or work in cities, is finding a time and place to walk. For some people, the only opportunity to get up and move their legs may be during their commute. I myself have been incorporating walking into my exercise regimen, and what I did was invest in a pedometer. This device allowed me to monitor and be conscious of how much I was able to get up and move my body on a day-to-day basis. I've made it a nightly routine before getting into bed to check my pedometer and write down how many steps I've accumulated that day.

I also measure and record my weight three times every day: in the morning and evening and at night. And I don't stop there, either. I also measure my body fat ratio to monitor the progress of my body's muscular development and the amount of fat I've lost, because an ordinary scale doesn't tell us these things. Sometimes, even though the scale keeps telling you the same number, your body constitution has changed. A stable weight could actually be hiding either an increase or a decrease in your body fat ratio. If your body fat ratio is increasing, it means that you're gaining fat and losing muscle, and if it's decreasing, it means you're losing fat and gaining muscle. I make an effort to be aware of the progress I'm making in my body constitution by making habit of monitoring these things.

I confess, I didn't do these things until I reached a certain turning point in my life. In the early stages of my career, I frequently traveled to speak to large audiences, and I found myself needing high-calorie meals, especially before these big events, to give me the energy I needed. Then, after the events, I would need to restore my energy again. In due course, this combination of a high-calorie diet and rest led me to gain weight.

When I realized what had happened to my body, I sought out a more health-conscious lifestyle. Since then, I have seen a significant transformation: my body has grown considerably leaner, I've improved my well-being, and I feel more vibrant than I did before.

Vitality of Body Fosters Vitality of Mind

This change in my attitude arrived in my forties as I began to notice changes in my body. These changes were the key that led me to become more conscious of my need to make lifestyle changes and begin taking measures toward preventive care. Until then, I had always been blessed with youthful vigor and a strong physical constitution and had never imagined that I'd ever fall ill. I knew then that I would have to change myself if I wished to serve my life's work into the evening of my life—and even more so if I wanted my twilight years to be healthful and zestful, so as not to become a burden to those around me.

This effort required some planning ahead and preemptive effort, of course, so I was inspired to begin the health and fitness regimen that I described earlier. Then, to maintain vitality and promote longevity, I knew that I would need to not only shed pounds and manage a healthy weight, but also make great strides in getting myself physically into shape. It became my goal, in the beginning, to walk ten thousand steps every day, and then I eventually moved on to incorporate muscle strengthening into my routine. I played tennis, swam, did indoor cycling for lower body training, and lifted weights for muscular training, among other forms of exercise.

The connection between our mind and body—physical fitness and mental vitality—isn't something we usually think to consider in our teens or twenties. But the passing of years eventually reveal to us all that staying in good physical shape is vital to keeping our intellect sharp and strong.

5

PREVENTING FATIGUE: THE UNEXPECTED SOLUTION TO LIFE'S PROBLEMS

Fatigue: The Root of Many Problems

We often don't think of tiredness as a serious issue. But we should caution against too easily brushing aside the signs of long-term bodily fatigue, because many of the problems we face in life can in large part be traced to the hampering effects of chronic tiredness. Noticing the wide impact of tiredness on the quality of many people's lives has led me to practice daily preventive measures to keep fatigue at bay. The difference fatigue makes in our lives is so great that I want to give special mention to preventing it, as one of the secrets to a healthful and happy life.

As long as we feel healthy inside—as long as each morning is an awakening into rejuvenation and breakfast is a pure delight—we'll see that it doesn't take much time to manage the problems we run into throughout the day. But on those days when we need to drag ourselves out of bed, breakfast feels bland, and we act grumpy around others, we are more likely to respond to our problems as though we are facing a crisis when they are in fact quite benign. This is the impact that tiredness has on the attitude we bring to the issues we handle on a day-to-day basis, and it shows us how important it is to our lives to consciously work to minimize the build-up of fatigue.

The Restorative Power of Five Minutes

What are some measures we can take to prevent long-term fatigue? My first piece of advice comes from understanding the natural restorative system within our bodies that fosters our ability to function optimally throughout the day. The natural renewing ability of our physiological systems is able to restore our energy when we give it proper rest.

The human mind cannot remain focused for longer than one hour at a time. Even the strongest-willed person will not be able to maintain the same level of concentration for longer than two or three consecutive hours, and past this threshold the mind's ability to stay focused begins to wane quickly. It  should come as no surprise, then, that our productivity drops between morning and night, particularly if our work consists of a lot of desk work, which has become a very common style of work today.

I'd say it's best to think of our mind's ability to stay focused as limited to about an hour at a time. And for our mind to continue working productively on our tasks throughout the day,

I really believe that we need to give our mind and body a break of about five minutes for each hour that we remain sitting and working. What this break does is to give our nerves an opportunity to unwind and relax after a span of, say, fifty-five minutes of intense work. I also recommend not being shy about giving ourselves some time during our lunch break to lie down if we can find a place to do so, or perhaps to at least find a sofa to relax in. Making a conscious effort to give ourselves this rest will serve our mind and body well and prevent fatigue from accumulating over time.

The Lower Back, Hips, and Feet: The Keys to Tireless Work

We build fatigue not only by overworking the mind, but also by overstraining the body. My second piece of advice to prevent chronic fatigue involves the care of certain areas of our body that serve an especially important role in fostering continuous activity and productivity over the course of a day.

First, we should be attentive to the health of our lower back and hips. Impairment or injury to this region of the body will inevitably diminish our ability to concentrate on our work and endure long hours of tenacious work. Setting aside some time each day to stretch and alleviate the strain will help prevent pain and injury to this area in the long term. Perhaps you can devote a few minutes of your lunch hour to stretching or doing some simple yoga positions that target the muscles in your lower back and hips. If time allows, I also highly recommend reclining on a sofa, which will allow your body to more fully relax and release tension.

Second, our feet are another part of the body that literally carry a heavy load. Each time we get up and walk, we are relying on the small surface area of the soles of our feet to carry around more than one hundred pounds of weight. The soles of our feet aren't made for bearing this kind of strain for longer than an hour, but many of us spend several hours a day on our feet. Finding a way to lie down will serve our feet well by giving them a break from the heavy load we put them through. With whatever other means we can find, we should make a conscious effort to care for the well-being of our feet by letting our body relax and unwind.

By being kind and attentive to these areas and freeing them from constant strain, we will be able to save two vital parts of our body from the effects of long-term fatigue.

Being Kind to Your Eyes Supports Your Intellectual Well-Being

We should also be kind to our eyes. Tiredness, when it sets into our vision, will affect our intellectual activity and digestive system. This in turn creates stress and anxiety that can give rise to victim-complex responses to the situations that arise in our day.

So what can we do to keep our vision from becoming overly fatigued? First, we should work in good, consistent lighting. Second, I recommend maintaining a distance of at least eight inches from your paper or screen. Third, I strongly advise

avoiding small writing. So if there are two edi-
tions of the same book—such as a paperback
edition and a hardcover edition—for instance,
it's better to choose the one with the larger
text, even if it turns out to be more expensive.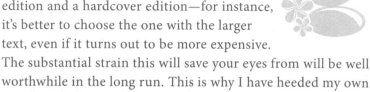
The substantial strain this will save your eyes from will be well
worthwhile in the long run. This is why I have heeded my own
advice and taken pains to use larger text in many of my books
to offer the least strain possible on my readers' eyesight.

We should always keep in mind that intellectual pursuits
inevitably challenge the health and longevity of our vision,
and the pains we take to care for our eyesight can never be too
much. Like our lower back, hips, and feet, our eyes can be
revived by giving them a break. We can do this simply by taking
our eyes off our work and resting our gaze upon something else.

Our eyes are naturally capable of long and continuous use,
as long as they get ample rest so they're not under constant
strain. Our vision is sure to falter if we strain our eyes by using
them for five to ten hours straight, but if we give them short
breaks every hour, they will last for eight to ten hours with ease.

In conclusion, I sincerely urge you to be kind to your body
and take great care to preempt the accumulation of fatigue in
your lower back, hips, and eyes for the longevity of your health
and well-being.

The Spiritual Truth
behind Brain Death

For some time now, medical professionals have been debating the condition of brain death, the cessation of the functions of the brain. Most of them now think of brain death as indicating that a patient has died. But when people see that the rest of the bodily functions remain in healthy condition even when the brain has stopped functioning, they may wonder whether that is so. I believe that by exploring brain death and the relationship between the mind and the brain from a spiritual perspective, we can gain a better understanding of the truth.

Having spent more than thirty years of my life as a spiritual teacher in devotion to the divine truths, and having experienced an awakening within my consciousness in 1981, I've learned a lot over the years about the spiritual aspects of our human existence. My awakening has blessed me with the gift of communicating with great figures in history who now reside in the other world. And since then, I have been publishing their manifold messages alongside my own work to give voice to their valuable ideas and philosophies for the benefit of others in this world.

These messages have had a big effect on how I understand the nature of life. I've seen that when these spiritual beings speak, they express sophisticated, well-developed thoughts with as much eloquence as anyone

in the flesh. And they even express the same philosophies, ideas, and habits that characterized them during
their life in this world. These messages have shown me
that while death may have taken these people's bodies,
their intelligence has not perished. And when I saw
that our conscious intelligence continues to exist in the
other world after death, I realized that the seat of our
intelligence lies not within the physical brain but within
the soul.

The physical brain's true purpose is not to help us
think but to serve as a control center or main computer to direct the other physiological functions of the
body. So the medical condition of brain death is just
an indication that the main computer has crashed and
frozen our physical ability to express our thoughts and
gestures. It is solely those functions that have been
lost—our conscious intelligence and thoughts remain
with our soul.

The soul and the physical body can be compared
to ourselves and our car; just as we are the driver with
conscious intelligence and the car is the purely mechanical vehicle, our souls are the part of us that thinks,
whereas our bodies are vehicles that carry us through
our life in this world. Therefore, just as we know that

an immobilized car is not a sign
that the driver inside has died,
even if it seems from the outside
as though the driver may have
stopped functioning, the condition

of brain death does not signify that we have deceased from this world. This also reveals to us that our mind and soul, not our brain or body, must be the parts of us that make us who we are.

This spiritual perspective allows us to also realize that even when we're in a condition when our brain fails to control speech and respond to stimuli, we are still wakeful and conscious inside, thinking real thoughts, feeling emotions, and listening to surroundings. In fact, the human soul houses a spirit body through which we are able to hear others' words spiritually and grasp their thoughts and feelings intuitively, even if we have lost our hearing. This is true not just in brain death, but also in other terminal illness.

It's my firm belief and sincere hope that gaining this spiritual awareness of the connection between the mind and body will shed light on the confusion we find today about brain death and what truly determines death.

CHAPTER 2

THE MIND-BODY SECRET TO HAPPINESS AND WELL-BEING

HEALING DISEASE BY HEALING STRESS

Stress Is the Underlying Cause of Many Internal Diseases

Today, we may find ourselves surrounded by a constant flood of information about the many causes of disease, which may leave us feeling confused and lost. While we are frequently reminded by medical experts that lack of exercise and overindulgence of food are major causes of health problems, I would like to point out a more basic cause underlying the large majority of human illnesses: stress. Stress is an especially common cause of internal diseases.

Most of us would like to bring harmony and balance to our day-to-day lives. But modern life often poses obstacles to our efforts to reduce stress, maintain inner calm, and practice the spiritually conscious, Truth-based lifestyle that we'd like to follow. The majority of us instead find ourselves practicing lifestyles within harsh vibrations, like those we find in the business world. We sometimes face a great deal of stress at work—for example, when we make a huge mistake that leads to strong censure from our superior. Or we may have been relying on a client's payment to bring in revenue and then be thrown into a frenzy when that payment doesn't arrive.

When we allow stress from situations like these to go on unhealed, the toll this takes on our mental health eventually causes imbalances and diseases within the body. How does this happen? To understand the mechanism of disease, it helps to begin by understanding the basic spiritual structure of the human body.

We each possess a spirit body that's identical to our physical body. Similarly, each internal organ, including the heart, kidneys, and intestinal tract, houses a spiritual counterpart that mirrors its shape and characteristics.

Our organs all have individual spirit bodies, because each of them holds a unique role of its own and is in charge of recognizing a different feeling or sensation. For instance, the digestive organs are keenly sensitive and especially adept at feeling and sensing. The heart holds a similar sensory role but is in charge of a larger scope of sensations. In this way, each of our organs' spirit bodies symbolizes a specific way of recognizing stress. When we are under a lot of stress, our first response comes from the spirit body of one of these organs. The damage from that stress will then manifest in the corresponding physical organ.

Spiritual Practices Can Prevent Cancer

By understanding how the mind and body work together, we can see how we develop diseases such as cancer: the physical form of cancer is preceded by a spiritual form of cancer that arises from stress within the mind. The damage caused by stress on the spiritual level nurtures an apposition of stress in the same place in the body, and this stress in turn manifests as disease.

Therefore, we can heal and prevent disease by healing our stress and harmonizing our mind. Though there are physical causes of disease, stress contributes far more to the growth of disease, and many more people find healing by dissolving the stress from their mind than by paying attention only to physical causes.

To heal and prevent stress, I recommend simple methods of mindfulness that enable you to fade stress and return harmony to your life. Two good methods are the practice of the teachings of love and self-reflection. Positive thinking and meditation are two more helpful practices. Happy Science, the organization I founded, offers many methods of meditation because meditation has been found to spread deep relaxation to our internal organs and nervous systems, which helps heal diseases, such as cancer, that affect these areas. For this reason, I highly recommend meditation to those who are on a journey to heal cancer or a similar disease.

FINDING HEALING THROUGH FORGIVENESS

Resentment and Hate Can Spawn Diseases

Some health conditions seem to have no clear cause, and we may wish that there were something we could do to promote healing. A cause can actually be found in most of these cases, and it often lies in our own pent-up feelings of hate or resentment. Hate and resentment weigh down our hearts and manifest as problems with our own health. By holding onto such feelings, we send them out into the world, where they create physical problems for the people we have these feelings for. But this burden falls upon ourselves as much as on them.

Often, underneath our hate and resentment lies an unwillingness to forgive. We may think to ourselves, "He did something unforgiveable" or "She doesn't deserve my forgiveness." As we carry such feelings within us, they begin to physically manifest as lesions within the body through a natural link that unites our mind and body. In some cases, allowing these damaging feelings to stay with us can cause the lesions to grow into cancer cells. The majority of us remain unconscious of these intimate dynamics between the mind and body, and the result is that we find diseases in this world that seem as if they have appeared for no clear reason.

Cancer Can Be Cured through Forgiveness

The cure, therefore, is to find forgiveness in your heart—for yourself and for others. When you look back on your life, you'll certainly find people who made you feel injured, humiliated, ostracized, and denigrated—and you'll probably find more than just a few of them. Finding the heart to forgive them in spite of their behavior will bring you to the path to healing. Sometimes we are apt to hold onto hate and resentment for a year, three years, or even as long as five years. If you have held onto hate and resentment for this long, you've suffered long enough.

Perhaps many of the people who hurt you have changed since then or felt ashamed and remorseful when they realized what they'd done. We all make mistakes from time to time, and they may have regretted their error the moment that they recognized it. These things are not at all unlikely, and if that's so, then it's hard to find any meaning in carrying on with your hate and resentment. Perhaps what they did brought you a lot of harm and caused you to suffer a lot of pain, but as we often find in this world, they are not perfect, just as you are not perfect. By letting go of your negative feelings and finding the will to forgive, I am certain that you will find healing.

THE SPIRITUAL RELATIONSHIP BETWEEN PAST LIVES AND ILLNESS

Our Past Lives Can Affect Our Present Well-Being

In some cases, an illness and its symptoms are the result of memories of a hard death we had to go through at one point or other in our past lives. This is not an uncommon phenomenon. The great anguish and hardship of this death, whether it resulted from tragedy or illness, get deeply impressed within our soul, and these memories unconsciously surface into our new life as a variety of health problems. The memory of hardship first affects the outer layer of our spiritual body, the astral body, and then manifests as a physical ailment.

Case 1: Birthmarks

We've all probably seen someone with a birthmark, or we may

have one of our own. Birthmarks that have a peculiar, bruise-like look to them are a remarkably accurate indication of the way the person died in a past life. Many people who were killed by a sword, spear, or arrow in a past life develop birthmarks in the location of their former wound, and many such cases have been reported. The birthmarks seem to serve as a poignant reminder of this experience.

Case 2: Skin Conditions, Asthma, and Bronchitis

I have taught before that skin-related problems are sometimes a sign of a strong allergy to a particular person or relationship. But in some cases, these conditions can be traced back to the way the person died in a past life.

For instance, skin-related problems often affect people who died in a fire. Their subconscious memories of the painful sensations they endured in that experience physically manifest throughout their body, developing into marks on the skin or breaking out into allergic reactions or other skin diseases. This condition is very widespread.

An experience like this can also manifest in the form of ailments such as asthma, bronchitis, or other respiratory diseases. These diseases mirror the agony of the smoke inhalation and suffocation that these people suffered. Through past life regression therapy, a treatment that uses hypnosis to recover the memories of a person's past lives, people who suffer from these illnesses have remembered dying this way. And simply by becoming consciously aware of this cause, they were able to heal their symptoms with striking results. Since the source of the illness was in the mind, they were able to heal themselves by resolving these issues within their mind.

Case 3: Fear of Water

We also hear a lot about nonphysical health conditions, such as the different phobias, which are essentially anxiety disorders. If you struggle with frequent bouts of aquaphobia, an abnormal fear of being in water, and suffer anxiety attacks any time you are near a pool, river, or any kind of body of water, your past-life reading would most likely reveal experience with drowning. Perhaps you were on a sinking ship, in an accident near a body of water, or caught in a flood; in any case, it's very likely that you met your death from drowning in a previous incarnation. This kind of experience may leave your soul with a strong feeling of unbearable fear, and this fear may sometimes manifest in your daily life. This is the source of your uncontrollable feelings of fear and your phobia.

Case 4: Fear of Heights

Perhaps an even more typical phobia is the fear of heights. If you are acrophobic, it feels impossible to control the onslaught of panic that overcomes you when you find yourself standing in a high place. You may have already guessed by now, but a past-life reading may reveal that you once died by falling from a height. You may have fallen from a cliff, a rooftop, a tower, or a high window. Some have experienced this in the midst of war or from being pushed. We've also seen, in recent years, people beginning to be diagnosed with an extreme fear of flying; this fear comes from their experience of meeting death in a plane crash.

We can see from these examples that our mind sometimes holds onto the fear we gained in previous incarnations as a type of karma, and that fear manifests in our present life as a phobia or anxiety disorder. We can also gather from this that historical changes will continue to spawn new forms of phobias. For instance, victims of car accidents may develop phobias of cars or vehicles in their next life (see the inset "Life Is Like a Workbook" at the end of this chapter).

Case 5: Fear of Being Closed In

A third common type of phobia is claustrophobia, the fear of enclosed spaces. This condition makes us feel suffocated when we enter a small room, elevator, or locked place, and this is a reaction we are apt to take on when we've died in such a place, with no way of escaping, in a previous life. If you are claustrophobic, a past-life reading would likely show that you went through this kind of experience in a previous incarnation. People who were victims of the Nazi gas chambers may develop claustrophobia and suffer a lot of fear of enclosed spaces. In cases like that, when many people were killed at once, a lot of them are born again quite quickly and are prone to developing symptoms of fear and anxiety attacks that reflect the way they recently died.

Some cases of claustrophobia can be traced further back in history to ancient Egypt. During some periods, ancient Egyptians followed a custom of including the handmaidens and servants of the deceased pharaoh with the treasures that were buried with him in his tomb. The Egyptians of that time believed that the pharaoh would do well to have his handmaidens and servants accompany him to the afterlife to help take care of his daily needs, so many of them were buried alive as offerings to the pharaoh. Many of them probably weren't ready to die yet, and this experience can lead to claustrophobia in the next incarnation as a karmic symptom of their souls' strong fear of being buried alive.

Case 6: Panic Attacks

Some cases of panic disorder could be a symptom of the profound panic and anxiety that a person experienced in a previous life during a deadly ambush that came on suddenly and without warning. For example, some people may have been attacked by bandits during a journey in the mountains, assaulted by thieves and killed in an alleyway, murdered in their home by burglars, or killed in some other kind of surprise attack.

If you suffer from spells of intense panic but can't seem to find an obvious, natural cause in any of your life experiences, even those from your early childhood, you'll most likely find the root of your panic attacks in one of your many previous incarnations. You'll also find more hints to help you overcome panic attacks in part II, chapter 1 "Overcoming Past Trauma."

AWAKENING THE POWER OF SELF-HEALING AND RENEWAL

We Are Blessed with the Power of Self-Healing

We human beings have been blessed with the power of regeneration. We are naturally able to restore our bodies to a state of perfect health and wholeness. But most of us have forgotten how to use this power, so our subconscious has kept it mostly unused and concealed. Most people today would be very skeptical to learn of this power. But many forms of life, including other animals, have the same power to self-heal.

Lizards and crabs, for example, have the ability to grow their tails and limbs back, just as we humans are supposed to be able to do with our limbs. This ability is needed by many living creatures, both human and animal, because our bodies are made up of parts that are essential for our survival. Crabs' claws are their indispensable tools for hunting food and fighting predators. They wouldn't be able to get on for long in the wild seas if their claws could never grow back after being severed or damaged.

When God imparted the crabs with this ability, the complexity of the claws' biological structure didn't matter to Him or to the crabs' own biological system. And this should also hold true with our own bodies. Could God, who blessed these creatures with this healing capacity, have denied this simple gift to us, His most cherished creations? I don't believe He would have denied the healing power of regeneration to the multitudes of people in this world who seek health and healing.

Perhaps it wasn't God who denied us, but we who have been denying ourselves by allowing materialism to pollute our beliefs about what we are truly capable of. Many doctors and medical professionals have convinced us that we have no control over our internal organs, explaining that they are composed of involuntary muscles that the human body cannot direct at will, unlike the voluntary muscles, which we can operate by our own volition.

This is what our biology textbooks also say about our bodies, so the majority of us have probably never thought to question whether it's true. But I am here to tell you that this is not at all the truth. Within every cell of our body—including those that construct our bones and the involuntary muscles that make up the internal organs—the process of change and recreation is constantly at work throughout our lives.

While the change may be more gradual for some parts than others, nothing in our body remains untouched by the power of change during our lifetime. The constant change that our body is undergoing means that we can direct our body toward healing and renewal at will. With a strong, unflagging will to do so, we can place the changes happening in our body under our own control, however gradually they may progress. For it is the influence of our own will that also creates cancer and other diseases in our body.

If we can use our will to bring ruin to our body, then we can also use it to guide our body toward health and healing. There are no exceptions to this capacity for self-healing. We can even heal and strengthen our heart, digestive tract, kidneys, and other internal organs. We can even strengthen our brain, though in this case we do so through education and diligent study.

Your Will Is the Key to Finding Healing

It truly serves us to believe that we can heal our own body. It may require time, but we will be able to find healing for certain as long as we hold the strong will to do so. And meanwhile, we also need to make practical efforts to improve the health of our body. Finding healing through a strong will isn't only about wishing for it to come to us; it is also about making the proper effort to make it a reality.

For instance, if you suffer from lung cancer, your body won't be able to get rid of the cancer if you continue to smoke a hundred cigarettes a day, no matter how strong your prayers are. That may be asking too much. You'll need to take measures to quit your smoking habit for your lung to be able to heal. Likewise, if your cholesterol has risen to unhealthy levels, you will need to do what you must to bring your cholesterol numbers down, such as eating less fatty foods and exercising more. Where there are clear actions that will effectively help you heal, you need to take those actions, as you hold in your mind a strong desire to heal your specific health problems. By doing both, your health will begin to steadily improve in the ways you desire. This is not anything to be surprised by. Healing happens to many people this way all the time.

Many people these days are getting braces to help straighten their teeth, but we do not actually need braces to do this. Even teeth can be moved if we continue to will them to move for, say, a whole year. If you want a tooth to move an eighth of an inch to the left, you can achieve this by persistently willing it to happen.

Similarly, God didn't create our bodies to be so susceptible to nearsightedness. We are actually capable of moving the lenses of our eyes to adjust our own vision. But many of us have chosen to wear glasses. This makes it difficult for our eyesight to improve, because the muscles around our eyes tend to adapt to the eyeglass lenses, ultimately weakening our eyes' ability to focus on their own.

Each part of our body has the potential for improvement and progress and, therefore, healing. With the help of time, there is nothing we cannot heal by combining practical steps with a strong will.

5

THE SPIRITUAL TRUTH BEHIND ORGAN TRANSPLANTS

Organ Transplants Can Cause Spiritual Possession

While organ transplantations do much to help save and prolong the lives of many people, these procedures entail serious risks when we don't take their spiritual aspects into full consideration as we make decisions about receiving an organ transplant or becoming an organ donor. We need to keep in mind an important metaphysical truth about our organs: our internal organs are not just physical objects. Each of them is also a living, transcendental entity with an individual consciousness of its own. Imagine what can happen, then, when a conscious organ is extracted from its original home and suddenly planted into a foreign body belonging to a complete stranger.

Let's explore what happens using a heart transplant as a hypothetical example. Our heart has an essential metaphysical role: it is the central hub of all our thoughts, emotions, and feelings, and it governs them. We all know that in a heart transplant, our heart is removed from us, the donor, and grafted into the recipient's body, but what most people don't know is that this procedure is often conducted before our soul has had enough time to absorb the shock of our death. In this situation, the most frequent result is a type of supernatural apposition of our spirit onto the living recipient, effectively producing a kind of medically induced spiritual possession between us and the recipient.

Why and how does this happen? When we die suddenly, our spirit naturally continues to feel a connection with our heart and so is drawn by the natural pull of the dislocated heart to the organ recipient's body. The result is the coexistence of two individual souls within the recipient's body. This phenomenon explains why many cases of transplant rejection, in which the recipient's immune system attacks the transplanted organ, have been reported to occur after these procedures.

Another important spiritual consequence of such procedures is the impediment they pose to our spirit's smooth passage to the other world: transplants often trigger distress, grievances, and emotional attachments to this world that motivate us to stay here. This impedes many spirits from making their way back to the other world; instead, they end up staying in this world as unhappy spirits who get attached to this world.

Lost spirits are prone to creating spiritual disturbances in this world and sometimes causing successive misfortunes and mishaps to organ recipients' families and households. This phenomenon is the same as the "curses" we're told about that have existed since ancient

times. Unfortunately, organ transplants have produced many "cursing," unhappy spirits in this world.

Modern Medicine Lacks a Spiritual Understanding of the Mind-Body Connection

When I see heart surgeons who are working zealously to encourage their patients to undergo heart transplants, I am often reminded of the ancient Mayan practice of human sacrifice. The Mayan civilization had a custom of performing human sacrifice to please the gods, and these sacrifices sometimes involved offering the gods the living hearts of those who were chosen to be sacrificed. It's been said that tens or even hundreds of thousands of human hearts were taken and sacrificed while the people were still alive to carry out these rituals.

Many of today's heart surgeons may have been the knife-wielding ancient Mayan priests who performed these rituals and made a profession out of removing tens of thousands of hearts. Perhaps a lot of today's heart surgeons are the reincarnations of these Mayan priests.

In light of all of these spiritual workings, including this ancient history, it seems that heart transplantations may not be so much a proof of true scientific advancement as they are a representation of medicine's regression toward ancient practices. Ironically, modern medicine's understanding of the human mind and body seems to have gotten stuck in the knowledge of an antiquated age. So it's my strong sentiment that today's medical practices will stay in an archaic stage of advancement until medical experts are able to unravel the secrets of the spiritual connection between the mind and body.

The spiritual form of the human body is capable of feeling pain, but most physicians today aren't yet aware of this fact. Physicians and medical experts haven't realized that the spirits of all their deceased patients continue to feel the sting of the IV needle that they were treated with during their final moments in the hospital. If physicians aren't able to learn and accept this spiritual truth, it may be beyond them to fathom the tremendous degree of pain that a person's spiritual body experiences during an organ removal procedure when the physical body is still really alive but in a state of brain death.

I hope that I have been able to shed some light on the obsolescent circumstances of the medical knowledge and practices that are accepted as truth today, to help spread spiritual awareness to the medical community and those who seek healing.

6

THE PURPOSE OF DEATH

Finding the Meaning of
This World and Death

We know somewhere in the depths of our hearts that our true home is in the spirit world—the place beyond this world—and so this world seems just an ephemeral shadow. But we believe, too, that this world must be not just a figment of our imagination but a purposeful place to foster the spiritual growth of our soul. This is our reason for taking on a physical body while we are here temporarily: it is our means for living and expressing ourselves as we carry on through this world.

And then, of course, we'll each reach a point in life when we'll relinquish our transient body and return to that world beyond as a soul. This is why we so often don't find lasting happiness in the pleasures that can only be enjoyed in this world.

The happiness we really want to attain in this life, then, is the kind that lasts—the kind we can take with us to the other world. This is the happiness of enlightenment.

We can explore, for example, the happiness that was sought after by Shakyamuni Buddha, who renounced the secular world and founded Buddhism. Shakyamuni Buddha by no means forsook his desire for happiness when he chose to renounce worldly life. In fact, according to Buddhist scriptures he remarked that no one had ever gone to the same lengths as he did in the pursuit of happiness. There was no doubt in Shakyamuni's mind that enlightenment was the source of the true happiness that he so desired to find.

Worldly pleasures and the satisfactions of the physical body inevitably fail to bring lasting happiness in life, for this world is a place of impermanence and constant change, and so the physical youth and beauty that embellish us now are not ours for eternity. Time, never discriminating, will bring to us all the inevitable declines of age, including wrinkles, gray hair, and a hunching back. And with further decline, time will also bring illness and the eventual conclusion of this life. This unchangeable truth is perhaps the one thing since Shakyamuni Buddha's time 2,500 years ago that has remained unchanged in a world of adamant impermanence. No one in his time could escape the natural course of birth, aging, illness, and death, and so it is with us to this very day.

Parting with Loved Ones Fosters Your Spiritual Growth

We have seen significant medical advancements and great strides in disease prevention and measures to extend human life. But even leading-edge advancements in science and medicine haven't succeeded in stopping human life's natural progress toward death. And instead, as a consequence, we may have created additions to the list of human sufferings that would have been unimaginable in the time of Shakyamuni. At that time, no one with a terminal illness had to lie in bed with numerous tubes and machines attached to his body for the sake of prolonging life. This "spaghetti syndrome" may be a very painful way of being alive, but it is nonetheless suffered by countless patients throughout the world today. It's as if we produced this new way of suffering in exchange for the chance to extend our time in this world.

This has happened because many people of this world and the medical community no longer believe in life after death and hold onto the view that this life is all we will ever have. It's important to strive to live as happily as possible in this world, and I am in full support of this perspective. At some point, however, there also comes a time when we'll need to humbly accept our fate as humans. We can liken ourselves to a student in elementary school who needs to progress onto higher grades. We might find our current school very joyful, but when we reach a certain age, the time will arrive when the next grade awaits us. In just the same way, this world is like a stepping stone that allows us to advance to the world after death to learn in a new place.

As a graduating sixth grader, we probably couldn't hold back our tears as we said good-bye to our classmates. In the same way, it's only natural to feel pain and sorrow at the thought of having to say farewell to our dear friends and family. But as human beings striving for growth, this experience is an invaluable part of our progress toward the next stage. It's in our destiny to move on to middle school, then to high school, and finally to college.

Death is, indeed, a parting from our beloved friends and family that may, of course, bring a lot of grief and heartache to both us and them, and there is no way to escape from this final rite of passage in the twilight of our life. But the journey of our death is similar to a transition to a carefully selected school that's best suited to our academic aptitudes and specific strengths and interests. When we die, we will move on to the place in the afterworld that best suits the accomplishments of our life and the unique traits of our soul, and many of our close friends will be waiting for us there. So it's not necessary to grieve over our departure from this world or to anguish about the separation from our friends and family. By accepting, in your heart, the transient condition of this world, you will find inner peace and hope to help you on your wondrous passage to the other world.

THE DISABLED AND UNFORTUNATE ARE BEACONS TO ALLAY OUR EGOS

They Remind Us to Cultivate a Heart of Humanity

I have seen many people in this modern age suffering from an illness that afflicts not their physical well-being or their psychological health, but the heart of their soul. The affliction I want to talk about comes from being blessed by such wealth and material abundance that it deceives us into somehow feeling privileged to treat others with contempt and disdain and proud enough to elevate our egos and ambitions.

Such people need to go back to the starting point of what it truly means to be human and to think about what the human heart really ought to be like. Many people in this world struggle under less fortunate circumstances, facing the hardships of illness, poverty, and disability. Their struggle must be truly great, and from them there are precious lessons to be learned by the rest of us. Through their example, they allow us to see how blessed we are to have been born into a financially stable upbringing and with nothing to permanently ail or disable our body.

Needless to say, their hardship is neither a sign of something inherently wrong with their soul nor punishment for some kind of error in their past, as was often believed to be the case in ancient India as part of the law of karma. Those who endure such hardships in affluent societies have come as our teachers to awaken us to the errors of our own hearts and deeds, and by doing so, they help us find our way back to the heart of humanity and beneficence. By serving as exemplars of the plight of human disability and unfortunate circumstances, they are fulfilling their true divine role as beacons of guiding light for those who live in this world.

They Are Angels of Compassion in Disguise

There are multitudes of children suffering from severe disabilities, people struggling with incurable diseases, and people trying to pull themselves out of the need for welfare assistance. Many of these people are fulfilling a mission to serve as angels of compassion in disguise, offering others the chance to awaken to their mistaken ideas. Some, like Helen Keller, have served as tremendous beacons of light for the world. And others have had a humbler influence as they have lived in poverty or suffered from other hardships to inspire those with an inflated sense of self-importance to awaken to their false views.

Sadly, many people throughout the world still aren't aware of the divine purpose of these angels. We can still find people who think nothing of disparaging and mocking the unfortunate, unaware that they are our precious teachers. This is indeed a regretful state for this world to be in. There is still a lot of progress to be made towards understanding what love truly is, on a deeper and more refined scale, and to grow the number of people who take it upon themselves to practice true, compassionate love for others.

Life Is Like a Workbook

We often say that we are all created equal. But we may wonder why there are such wide discrepancies from person to person in terms of our lot in life. We're different not only externally, in our life circumstances, but also internally, in our natural aptitudes.

How do these discrepancies come about? The differences we find in everyone's lives didn't suddenly appear in our present lives. Our souls have been following a system of reincarnation throughout eternity. We've revisited this world countless times, each time gaining experiences for our spiritual growth. The sum result of these unique experiences influences us in our present lives, giving each of us a life that's unique. This concept is similar to the law of karma, a philosophy that has gained wide appeal today and that some ancient cultures used to try to explain the differences in our circumstances.

The philosophy of karma is supposed to acknowledge advantages as much as disadvantages, but it seems that, traditionally, the disadvantages have been emphasized more often. For example, the concept of karma explains that others hurt us in this life because we hurt someone else in a past life, that we were born blind in this life because we caused someone else to lose eyesight in a past incarnation, or that we suffer chronic pain in our leg because we injured someone else's leg in a past life. Based on this philosophy and the spiritual law of causality, people believe that the bad karma that we reaped in our previous lives accumulates and manifests in the circumstances of this life.

If we conducted past-life readings, I am certain we would find this to be accurate to some degree. When we think of our life as a workbook of problems to solve, the problems that especially stand out from the others are often the ones whose ultimate cause lies in our experience in one of our past lives.

But we should be careful not to oversimplify the philosophy of karma. It is not just a law of punishment or retribution for sins or bad deeds. There are, indeed, cases in which someone who has committed murder may have to become the victim in a next life. But the purpose of the law of karma isn't to punish. Often, it's we ourselves who choose to incorporate such experiences into our life plan when we determine to be born into this world again. In many cases, we voluntarily choose severe circumstances for ourselves, because we hope that by doing so, we'll be able to truly understand the sufferings of the victims of our misdeeds in previous lives.

In this sense, gaining a right understanding of the law of karma can help us accept the disadvantageous circumstances of our present life. Each time we lay out

 our life plan before we are born to this world, we purposely plan for our life not to be smooth sailing all the time. We sometimes choose harsh circumstances and conditions to give our soul opportunities to evolve and grow so that it can become the best soul it can possibly be.

Part II

Answering Questions
on Healing from Within

CHAPTER 3

CURES FOR THE SOUL

SPIRITUAL REMEDIES FOR MILD DEPRESSION

QUESTION

What are the spiritual causes and cures for mild depression?

ANSWER

When we feel down, we attract various kinds of spirits and often come under spiritual influence. The first spiritual law we should know in such cases is that we can only be influenced or possessed by spirits that are on the same spiritual wavelength as we are. Supernatural beings with no spiritual connection to us cannot come to us. The fundamental rule of the spirit world is that only spirits with similar vibrations or tendencies can connect with one another.

So studying the type of spirits that come to us will help us see where within our mind the problem lies. If you feel that you may be on the receiving end of spiritual interference, look within and check to see if you have any thoughts or feelings that may have attracted these spirits.

Remedy #1: Calmly Reflect on Your Mind

The most effective way to drive out negative spirits is to practice self-reflection. Calm introspection is the best thing to do when you are under negative spiritual influence.

How can we tell if we are experiencing such spiritual interference? The most typical symptom is the tendency to blame others. If, when things don't go as you expect, you find within yourself thoughts such as, "It was all her fault" or "He is all wrong," take a moment to carefully examine whether these thoughts are really your own. Calm your mind and ponder deeply whether they emanate from deep within you or whether an invisible existence with these negative tendencies is making you think this way.

When something happens that makes you lose your temper and want to put all the blame on others, recover your composure and examine your mind to see whether you have any negative thoughts or feelings lurking within. If you do, look within to examine your thoughts and feelings and remove, one by one, the negative thoughts that have clouded your mind. It may take some time to do this, but thorough self-reflection can be truly empowering. This type of introspection is one way to remove negative spiritual influences that are making you feel depressed.

Remedy #2: Quietly Wait for Time to Pass

Another way to deal with mild depression is to quietly wait for things to improve. When everything seems out of kilter and nothing you do seems to work, continuing to struggle and pressure yourself to do something to get out of your depression may just further entangle you in its emotional trap.

Spiritual disturbances caused by negative sprits often do not last long. This is because they sooner or later have to return to the place where they belong: hell. Hell is a world of resentment, victim mentality, and malice against others. Although it is possible for the inhabitants of hell to temporarily possess people on earth, they always leave the person they are possessing in due course because staying in the vibrations of the physical world, which are discordant with the vibrations of hell, is a difficult toil for them.

Just as these negative spirits can make your life difficult, you can also make their life harder. Seeking the right mind can especially make the possessing spirits suffer considerably. Keep this in mind when you feel that you are under negative spiritual influence. These spirits suffer as much as you do, and they will leave you before long.

Even if you don't have the higher awareness necessary to know whether spiritual disturbance is the cause of your depression, negative spirits usually can't influence you for longer than three months, and their influence rarely lasts longer than six months, as long as you are leading a decent, regular lifestyle. Often, the negative spirits bothering you will go away within six months, and your mild depression will come to an end.

The spirits cannot remain with you over an extended period of time, because their "friends" from hell will come to bring them back to their world once they notice that they are enjoying their time away from home. So, another way to heal mild depression is simply to wait for time to pass. You may worsen your condition or even bring harm to your spiritual well-being if you randomly use quaint approaches or unusual methods in an effort to heal your depression yourself. So I recommend waiting calmly for your condition to improve. If you are willing to wait half a year, I'm sure that things will eventually change for the better.

Remedy #3: Brace Yourself for the Worst

Another way to cure mild depression is to practice positive thinking. Negative thoughts, if they are consistent and persistent, can put us in a prison of our own making. Those who suffer from a mild depression caused by negative spiritual influence tend to overreact to the slightest hint of trouble, treating it as if it is a huge problem. To them, the tiniest misfortunes often seem like a matter of life and death—an event as big as a catastrophic disaster.

If you feel that you have this tendency and often find yourself assailed by feelings of panic, try finding peace of mind by thinking of the worst-case scenario. If the worst thing that could happen to you is to lose your life, tell yourself that even if you lose your physical body, your soul will continue to exist. When we believe in the truth that human beings have eternal life, we will know that nothing can take away our life or our soul.

Because loss of life is often people's biggest fear, overcoming this fear can give us the strength to face any lesser fears about issues such as family troubles, relationship troubles, or job insecurity.

Knowing that you have eternal life, which no one can ever take away from you, what's the worst possible thing that could happen to you? Think about it and brace yourself for it. If you can prepare yourself and feel that you will be able to survive the worst possible situation that you can think of, then you will be able to maintain your calm no matter what comes your way.

If you bide your time prepared for any crisis, you will soon see silver linings in life. You will start noticing the good things that are happening to you. You may have felt as if only bad things happened to you, but it is simply not possible that only bad things happen in someone's life. If you prepare yourself to wait six months for something good to happen, you will see a favorable outcome within a month or possibly even within two weeks, so make the most of it when it comes.

If you feel depressed as a result of constantly battling with your shortcomings and failures, I suggest practicing positive thinking. Focus only on your positive aspects, and look at the bright side of life. Keep a close eye on any good things that are happening to you, and grow these seeds of happiness into a tree of happiness. Increasing feelings of happiness can dissipate unhappiness just as light dispels darkness.

These are my three recommendations for curing mild depression caused by negative spiritual influences.

Helping Others Recover from Mild Depression

How can we help others who are struggling with this problem? The first and probably the most effective way to help them is to compliment their positive aspects and strengths. You will most likely worsen their condition if you criticize their shortcomings or blame them for their failures and mistakes. So talk to them with a cheerful tone, and mention good things about them.

It is also good to create a peaceful and friendly atmosphere and embrace them with love. This feeling of supporting one another with friendship or fellowship is actually the key to conquering evil. Even those who are not strong enough to defeat evil spirits on their own can defeat them with the protection and help of friends.

As long as we continue to focus on the dark side, we will keep on thinking of negative things that make us unhappy. But the moment we decide to turn our gaze on the positive aspects of life, we will find that we are surrounded by happiness. I hope that many people will find the seeds of happiness in their lives.

HARMFUL EXTREMES OF DIETING

QUESTION

Some people, especially young women today, go on crash diets to lose weight. Could extreme dieting harm our spiritual well-being?

ANSWER

Regular dietary practices to keep fit are beneficial to our spiritual well-being, so there should be nothing to worry about with those. But going to extremes, for example by significantly cutting out food and drink, can invite starving inhabitants of hell to come haunt us.

Young women today tend to equate slimness with beauty, and many of them try to lose weight by frequently skipping meals and surviving only on salads and juices. They often become thin as rails so that they can wear slim-fitting clothes. But some of them rebound from dieting and overeat; even if they lose twenty pounds, they may end up gaining forty pounds. People who frequently swing back and forth from weight loss to weight gain are most likely under negative spiritual influences. In other words, they are possessed.

Mindful Dieting Can Protect You from Negative Influences

Hell is inhabited not only by human souls, but also by animal souls. Animals that didn't die of natural causes but instead died in an accident, starved to death, or fell prey to another animal can find it difficult to return to heaven and instead end up in the shallow levels of hell where animal souls reside. Most of them starved to death or were attacked and killed by predators.

Some animal souls yearn to be near human beings and so come out of hell and approach people in this world. They find a way to possess those who are abnormally obsessed with food—often young children. Those who are affected by animal souls and fall under their influence develop morbid appetites.

To cure an eating disorder, I suggest studying and practicing the teachings of Happy Science to cultivate a cheerful and happy heart and self-control, or the power to take control of a strong urge to eat. People suffering from eating disorders can also improve their condition by disciplining themselves and striving to correct their lifestyle habits so that they lead a diligent life. They should also try to control their eating so that they're consistently eating a reasonable amount of food.

Weight-loss diets, if done properly and sensibly, should not have any negative effects. But extreme dieting can make us susceptible to possession by animal souls and other evil spirits.

Spiritual possession can be the cause of peculiar behaviors such as gorging on food in the middle of the night and vomiting afterward, along with other abnormal eating habits. Someone who repeats this kind of behavior is most likely possessed by either an animal soul that has fallen to the hell of hungry spirits or a human soul that has starved to death.

If you are on a diet and notice that you're developing odd behaviors, or if someone close to you, such as a family member, tells you that you have detrimental eating habits, that's a sign that you need to straighten out your lifestyle. Mindful practice of self-restraint, diligence, and discipline will free you from any animalistic control.

CURING SLEEP PARALYSIS

QUESTION

Nightmares and sleep paralysis often wake me up in the middle of night. What can I do to sleep peacefully all night long?

ANSWER

Nightmares that distract us from sleeping at night are most likely caused by evil spirits. Likewise, if you experience sleep paralysis, in which you are conscious but unable to move at all, or if you feel as if someone is pressing down on your chest, evil spirits may be meddling with you. Let me offer some steps you can take to free yourself from these conditions.

Step #1: Pray

The first step is to ask for heaven's help through prayer. Members of my organization, Happy Science, can seek help from me, Happy Science's supporting spirit group, and their guardian spirits by reciting the prayers, "Words of Truth: The Dharma of the Right Mind," "Prayer to the Lord," "Prayer for Exorcising Evil Spirits," and "Prayer to Guardian and Guiding Spirits."

In addition, if you can move your hand, the best thing to do is turn on the light and sleep with the light on. Evil spirits find it easier to enter a dark room, so you can prevent them from coming in by leaving the lights on.

Another effective way to drive away evil spirits is to play one of my lectures on an audio player. This will help you sleep peacefully without being distracted by evil spirits, whether they habitually stay with you or only happened to attack you by chance.

Step #2: Practice Deep Breathing

A second thing to try when you just cannot move your body is taking a deep breath. Calm and conscious breathing will help you regain control of your own spirit.

You don't have to sit up to do this. While lying down, try to breathe in deeply using the lower abdomen below the belly button. This will allow fresh oxygen to come in and circulate through your body. Strangely enough, breathing in abdominally several times will make evil spirits leave you.

This actually has to do with one of the secrets of deep breathing; when we breathe in air, we simultaneously let God's light enter our body. When this happens, possessing spirits fall away from our body or loosen their hands and let go of us so that they're no longer holding us down. Practicing this breathing method can help you free yourself from sleep paralysis.

Step #3: Practice Positive Thinking and Self-Reflection

The third step is to shift your mindset toward positive thinking. Evil spirits can exert a controlling influence on us when the vibrations of our mind are in tune with those of the evil spirits. So we can cut ties with them by holding completely opposite thoughts. Dispel all negative thoughts and feelings from your mind, and fill your mind with happy, positive thoughts.

Another method is to practice self-reflection. Even if your chest is weighed down, preventing you from moving your body or hands, your mind is free to think. So while you are lying down, reflect on your thoughts. If you are suffering from sleep paralysis, it probably means that something happened during the day that disturbed your mind. So mentally review your day and examine your thoughts. Perhaps you had difficulty in your human relationships; for example, you may dislike someone and you may have had thoughts such as, "I can't stand him," or "I wish she weren't around." If this is the case, engage in self-reflection about your relationship with this person. You can start by mentally apologizing to this person for thinking negatively about him or her.

Step #4: Practice Gratitude

Another step is to feel grateful for your life. If, as the phrase goes, you live each day as if it were your last, it is as if your entire life is coming to an end every day. So imagine that the time has come for you to leave this world and return to a world of bliss. As you look back, remember all the good things that happened to you during your lifetime on earth. If you can feel happy and satisfied with your life and filled with gratitude, you will feel ready to die and return to the other world. Feeling grateful for the life you have lived will make the evil spirits feel ridiculous and make them want to leave you. This is an effective way to get rid of negative spiritual disturbance.

The next time you suffer from nightmares or sleep paralysis, I suggest trying out taking these four steps to rid yourself of evil spirits. Only those with spiritual powers can actually feel the presence of evil spirits and exorcise them. But even without spiritual powers, we can still practice expelling evil spirits in our dreams. If you have a bad dream, feel something pressing down on your chest, or find yourself unable to move at all, you'll know that evil spirits have come to you. Try each of the steps I have explained in this section. Before completing the last step, you will find your problem solved and will be able to go back to sleep peacefully.

MAINTAINING EMOTIONAL STABILITY DURING MENSTRUAL PERIODS

QUESTION

Some women become emotionally unstable during menstrual periods. How can we gain better control of our mind when we are on our period?

ANSWER

Women shoulder the "burden" of menstruation because this experience offers them precious lessons for their soul growth. This is not about menstruation alone; menstruation is part of the bigger process of bearing and raising children, which includes giving birth, nursing, and caring for children.

Some women may feel that they are in a disadvantaged position when it comes to childbearing. During pregnancy, they have to carry a baby in their womb for about nine months, and this prevents them from working at their full potential.

Furthermore, it takes almost twenty years for a child to become a fully grown adult. Among animal species, human beings take the longest time to reach maturity. Most baby animals can stand on their legs shortly after birth and reach adulthood within a year or so. But it is part of God's plan for human beings to take twenty years to reach adulthood. This system is designed to show that childbearing and child-rearing are sacred work and that God trusts women to fulfill this momentous undertaking.

Childbearing and Child-Rearing Promote Soul Growth

The question of whether this system is fixed and unchangeable may deserve further consideration, and there may be other styles or approaches we can take to producing and raising offspring. But the existence that created this mechanism thought that it would be beneficial to the growth of human souls.

Women may feel greatly inconvenienced by this system, but we can find within it the Creator's wish for women to become aware of their sacred task of sustaining the human species by experiencing the distresses, difficulties, and physiological anxiety that accompany it.

If women didn't menstruate and could give birth to children instantly and easily as a reptile lays eggs, it might relieve them of the physiological burden that causes distress and anxiety. But at the same time, they might also lose their sense of the sacred responsibility of bearing and nurturing new life.

Physiological Conditions Affect Our Emotional Stability Regardless of Gender

It is not only menstruation that can cause emotional instability. We tend to get emotional when we are feeling under the weather, too. In fact, very few people stay emotionally unaffected when they fall ill. Mood swings are not specific to women; men also experience mood swings when they are not in good physical condition. Catching a cold makes them feel weak, whereas recovering from it restores their mental stability.

No one can be free from physiological responses. We cannot completely avoid the disadvantages of residing in a physical body as long as we live in this world. What's important is that we shift our mind to minimize the harm that physiological conditions can cause.

Women's Spiritual Aptitude Helps Them Develop Sensitivity and Perceptiveness

If we look at it from a negative perspective, menstruation may seem like an inescapable burden. But we can also take a positive view. Any emotional instability that menstruation causes can help women develop sensitivity and grace. Menstrual periods can be good opportunities for deep introspection. Furthermore, the fact that a child's soul can dwell in the mother's body during pregnancy shows that women are far more spiritual than men.

Men can get by without having anything to do with spirituality; they may only need to worry about issues relating to their job. But the fact that women are born with the capability to conceive a baby and to nurture another soul within their body for about nine months shows that all women have an aptitude for developing psychic abilities. In this sense, all women are naturally psychic mediums. This is probably one of the biggest differences between men and women. Not all men can develop supernatural forces and become sensitive to spiritual influence, but all women are innately capable of developing spiritual powers.

The other side of the coin is that their spiritual susceptibility often causes emotional instability. But if you look at the positive side, women are deeply spiritual, which lets them develop sensitivity and understanding of other people's feelings and also a perceptiveness that enables them to appreciate art, beauty, and literature. I believe that when we talk about issues specific to women, we should focus on discovering the advantages of being a woman.

OVERCOMING PAST TRAUMA

ANSWER

Trauma and phobias have been the subjects of research and study in the field of psychology over the past century. However, as far as I can tell, strong psychological reactions often have roots that stretch deeper than the experiences of this lifetime alone.

Childhood experiences, such as violence and sexual abuse, can certainly trigger phobias, so it's not entirely wrong to find the cause of current phobias in the events of early life. But based on my own investigations and research, the roots of various phobias can be traced back to experiences in their former incarnations. So without a spiritual reading of the person's past lives, it is often difficult to pin down the real cause.

Memories of Your Past Lives May Be Affecting You Now

An intense experience in a past life, such as dying on the battlefield, being foully murdered, or dying from a severe illness or freak accident, often affects our emotional state in our current life. For example, someone who died in a flood will have a fear of water. Someone who was killed in a sneak raid and was suddenly and indiscriminately murdered on the street might suffer from unknown fears.

Memories of unfortunate events in past lives remain within our souls. We may have fallen a victim to an earthquake, been killed by falling rocks, died of the plague, or been killed in ambush. Psychology cannot always explain the real reasons for their fears; spiritual investigation is necessary to learn exactly what kinds of past-life experiences may be affecting us now.

Finding Happiness in the Present Can Change Your Past Experiences

On many occasions, I have taught that we cannot change what happened in the past, but we *can* change the future, so we should do what we can do to change our future. But there's more to this. In a way, we can change our past by changing the present. We see past events through the lens of the present. If you are happy now, all the events in your past become reasons for your present happiness. Do you see what I am trying to say?

If you are happy now, past misfortunes such as illness, bankruptcy, and lost love will transform into seeds of your present happiness. You will recognize that everything was meant to happen so that you could find happiness now.

But if you're unhappy now, you can easily come up with any number of reasons for your current unhappiness. It may be an illness that ruined your life. You may be unhappy now because you failed a test or your family went bankrupt. It could be because your boyfriend dumped you or because your father abused you when you were little. It could be because your parents used to beat you up or because your brother used to kick you around.

Even if you feel that you are unhappy because of what happened in the past, by choosing to become happy right here and now, you will see everything turn into sparkling, wonderful memories. This is how you can change your past. By changing your present self, you can change how you see your past self.

Some business tycoons attribute their financial success to poverty in early life. They feel glad to have been poor when they were young, because their strong wish to escape poverty was the driving force for the  hard work and perseverance that made them who they are today. They even appreciate the fact that their family struggled financially, because if their family had been rich, they probably would not have become as successful as they are. They feel this way because they are happy now.

If you are looking in the past for reasons for your current unhappiness, you may not have seen how this works. By filling your present self with light, you will be able to change how you see your past.

You may have no trouble finding misfortunes, failures, and mistakes that made you unhappy, but you can also transform them into seeds of happiness. Exploring your past and discovering what has made you the way you are today is one way to find guidance in life. But better yet is to see everything in your past in a different light simply by changing yourself right now.

Not only can we change our past in this lifetime; we can also change painful experiences in our past lives into the seeds of our present happiness. We have the power to be able to go back that far in time to turn our life around. If we have the power to change the past, changing the future shouldn't be that difficult. We can freely create our future with our own hands.

UNDERSTANDING GENDER IDENTITY DISORDER

QUESTION

One of my friends has gender identity disorder, and the gap between his biological sex and the gender he identifies with is constantly tormenting him. Could you give him advice and guidance for coping with this issue?

ANSWER

Gender identity disorder is an issue that has gained increasing attention recently, and it often has to do with the gender of the soul.

Human souls can be categorized into three types based on their style of reincarnation: the first type consists of souls that are repeatedly born as men. The second type is those who choose to be repeatedly born as women—many goddesses belong to this group. The third type takes turns being born in each gender. Those who don't feel at home with their gender often belong to the first and second types; they had been consistently born as male or female but were born in the opposite gender this time around. In other words, they are a bit in a shock because their physical gender is in discord with the gender of their soul. In most cases, this happened due to some error in their planning for the current incarnation before they were born into this world.

For example, let's say that you chose your parents before you were born, and you were absolutely determined to be their child. But if this couple decides to have only one child who turns out to be a girl, you may have no choice but to be born into a female body, even if it's against your wish to be born male. And it may be too late when you realize that it wasn't part of your plan to be born as a woman, and thus you may end up feeling perplexed about what to do.

Some people make perfect life plans before they are born into this world, but often, people with gender identity disorder were slack in planning their life before they were born. Most of them probably miscalculated and ended up being born in the opposite-gender body. These people feel strong gender dysphoria simply because their souls recognize themselves as the opposite sex. So in your friend's case, I think that somewhere along the line, there was an unexpected change in his life plan.

Coping with the Difficulty of Being Born into the Wrong Gender

What do you think happens to our gender when we return to the other world? Do souls have a gender? Those who lived as a woman in this world will usually retain the consciousness of a woman in the other world as well, until they are ready for the next incarnation. Similarly, most men will keep a male consciousness.

Today, many contemporary issues complicate the reincarnation process. There are many cases of abortion, and some people end up marrying someone other than the person they originally planned to marry, which may force unborn souls to change their plans. So things may not always go as planned.

But most of the souls who were born in a different gender than they planned find a way to cope with the situation. It is easier for them if their soul group consists of mixed-gender souls. And even if it is their first time being born male or female, they may gracefully accept the situation and live with it.

During the numerous cycles of reincarnation, most souls alternate being born male and female. This is because we cannot develop our full potential as a soul unless we accumulate experiences in both genders. But when souls that belong to a group consisting of all female or all male souls are born into the opposite sex, they sometimes have difficulty coping with the situation. In your friend's case, too, it seems as though his female soul just cannot accept dwelling in a male body. He probably cannot help feeling that something is wrong.

Although it may not have been your friend's plan to be born a man this time, this could still well be a valuable experience for his soul. So one option is to decide to live with it for the sake of gaining a new experience. If he just cannot accept the fact that he was born with the opposite gender, another option would be to have gender reassignment surgery.

Life Doesn't Always Go Your Way

The modern medical world does not recognize the spiritual causes of gender identity disorder, so they diagnose it as a malady. But from a spiritual standpoint, this is not a "disorder." These people are simply clearly conscious of their own sexual nature.

If you can let your friend know this spiritual truth of his condition, then it's entirely up to him how he would like to live his life. It would not benefit him to live his whole life resenting his biological sex, so he should sooner or later make a decision as to what he wants to do.

After all, we cannot have everything we want in the way we want it. Countless people feel distressed because things didn't turn out as they wished or their life took a completely different course from what they planned before they were born. Some may be unhappy because they are too tall or too short or too heavy or too skinny. Others may be disappointed with how they look or how unintelligent they are. We all live with a lingering feeling that something is not right. Everyone is struggling with an issue that they have difficulty dealing with, so I would like those with gender identity disorder to know that they are not the only ones suffering. I sincerely hope for the best for those struggling with this issue.

Soul Siblings and Spiritual Memories

Under most circumstances, a soul group consists of six soul siblings and is responsive to one core soul. This represents the central point, the command center of the soul, which shares its essence with five other soul siblings. All the soul siblings experience life, one after another. Each takes its turn at being born into different lives, and the soul thereby acquires different personalities. When soul siblings return to the spirit world after death, most tend to retain the appearance they had during their time as corporeal beings. When the soul siblings eventually come together, however, they still represent one complete soul. Each soul sibling knows that it is one component of the whole and that it and the other siblings together form one unique human soul. In each soul, therefore, a multitude of memories and experiences supplied by each component part overlap and converge.

ABORTION FROM THE SPIRITUAL PERSPECTIVE

QUESTION

If we create a life plan in heaven before we are born into this world, what happens to a soul that is aborted and is unable to be born as planned?

ANSWER

Most people who choose to have an abortion do so because they are unaware of the spiritual truth of the system of reincarnation.

Abortions have caused a lot of trouble and created confusion in heaven. There have been many cases in which people with important tasks were aborted, preventing them from fulfilling their mission in this world. Even spirits in heaven are unable to control the people on earth or force them to think or act in the way heaven wants. This is because God gave human beings the free will to choose for themselves the actions we take.

For example, in the spiritual interview I had with Murasaki Shikibu, an eleventh-century Japanese novelist and poet and the maid of honor of the Imperial Court, she said that she had planned to be reborn in the present age but she couldn't because she had been aborted.* In her case, her wish clashed with the free will of her intended parents on earth, and these people were more determined to carry out their decision than she was.

Abortion Causes a Setback for the Unborn Soul

Today, the reported number of abortions in Japan alone is close to three hundred thousand cases annually. Including the unreported cases, it is said that the actual number could be as high as one million. This has wreaked havoc in heaven and ruined the life plans of many souls who were preparing to be born into this world.

These souls carefully worked out the details of how they were going to spend the next several decades of life. When they get aborted while they are in their mothers' wombs, this experience inflicts a wound on the soul. This hurt develops into the fear that the same thing may happen again the next time they prepare themselves to be born into this world.

If a baby dies after it is born and takes a first breath of the air, and if a fetus dies after it has grown big enough to have its own will, it will have to return to the other world as the soul of an infant. The infant soul cannot immediately regain its original consciousness; it takes about twenty years for the soul to become an

---

* Ryuho Okawa, *Okawa Ryuho Reigen Zenshuu Dai 14 Kan* ["Ryuho Okawa Spiritual Message Collection Volume 14"] (Tokyo: Happy Science, 2001).

adult consciousness. This infant soul needs care and support from other spirits who have spiritual ties with the soul from infancy until it grows up enough to regain its original state of adult consciousness. This is a great setback for the evolution of the soul, and that's why I believe that abortion should be avoided as much as possible.

However, there may be times when economic, physical, or other conditions leave no other alternative. For example, abortion may be unavoidable if the childbirth would cost the mother's life due to her frail health. In life-threatening cases like this, they may have to regretfully abort the pregnancy. If they do, it is critical that the parents offer sincere prayers for the infant soul to grow up and mature to become an adult consciousness and to heal the wound that the abortion might have caused it. I believe that this is the least they can do for the unborn soul.

In principle, we should avoid abortions, but when they become absolutely necessary, we should remember to pray for the happiness of the unborn soul. At the same time, however, it is also important not to become too obsessed about it.

What Causes Viruses to Spread?

No matter how much research is done on medical treatment for existing diseases, new diseases keep emerging one after another. For instance, even if we find a cure for the HIV virus or AIDS, a new and different life-threatening disease will soon emerge as if to take its place.

AIDS was first recognized in the early 1980s and quickly became known as a new epidemic. The truth is that the same spiritual influence behind the spread of the plague in the fourteenth century and cholera in the nineteenth century is now acting on the AIDS virus. After the plague and cholera had gradually subsided thanks to advances in medical science, the spirits that affected them slowly transformed and eventually manifested as AIDS. So to better understand how diseases spread, we need to take into account the spiritual elements that affect pathogens.

The way we catch a cold or the flu is very similar to the way spiritual possession takes place. The same principle seems to be at work in both cases. Many of us have had the experience of developing cold symptoms such as coughs and a thick head shortly after meeting someone who had a cold. With spiritual sight, you would see the phenomenon of spiritual possession; the spirits are causing the spread of colds and flu.

What kinds of spirits do you think these are? Colds and the flu start spreading when the weather gets chilly. Can you think of creatures that die and become spirits at that time of year? They are actually spirits of insects and bugs. Autumn insects die off when winter arrives and the weather quickly cools down, and that is also when colds and flu become prevalent. These dead insects often become wandering spirits, gathering together in large groups and swarming about in the air. These insect spirits are what spread colds and influenza.

Viruses and bacteria are still the agents that carry diseases, but in themselves, they are not that harmful. They become contagious only when spiritual influences act on them. In other words, viruses spread when insect spirits possess them. This is the truth of viruses and diseases.

If you come to think of it, you would probably find it odd that viruses become rapidly contagious in winter, although viruses are alive all year around, even in spring and summer. This is because viruses increasingly gain force during the winter months when they come under spiritual influences of dead bugs and insects. Similarly, spiritual influence is the real reason for hay fever. Hay fever is often triggered by the pollen of cedar trees. This pollen causes a severe allergic reaction because of the spirits of dead trees and plants. Many mountain trees and plants have been cut down to build golf courses and other facilities, and their spirits cause hay fever.

Diseases that spread rapidly, whether it is the plague, cholera, AIDS, or the flu, are all under spiritual influence. So even if we find effective cures for these diseases, new ones will keep emerging until we eliminate the root cause. I believe that knowing this spiritual truth will help us find real cures for contagious diseases.

CHAPTER 4

TREATMENTS FOR DISEASES AND DISORDERS

THE CAUSES AND CURES OF ATOPIC DERMATITIS

QUESTION

I have a son with eczema. I have tried everything, from taking him to see the doctor to watching what he eats, but his condition isn't improving. Are there any spiritual remedies for atopic dermatitis?

ANSWER

To find the spiritual cause of atopic dermatitis, we need to first consider what kinds of issues that trouble the mind the skin disease may be representing. What state of mind might cause harm to our skin?

The skin is the outer layer of the body that separates the inside of the body from the outside. So skin abnormalities are often a sign of a disconnection between what's inside and outside.

What then do "inside" and "outside" represent? They represent our ego or soul and our relationships with others. For young children, the inside may be their family, while the outside may be everyone outside the home. In other words, the skin serves as a border between the self and others or between the family and the outside world.

A problem with this boundary line, that is, a rejection of the outside world, often causes atopic dermatitis. Those who reject the outside world often fear that they will be harmed by others, and their extreme reaction to this anticipation manifests as eczema.

Building Harmonious Relationships with Others Will Help Improve Skin Conditions

Children often develop atopic dermatitis when their family members strongly reject or feel rejected by the outside world. In your case, too, I believe that someone in your family may be causing your son's condition. I suggest that you consider whether anyone in your family, including yourself and your spouse, spiritually has a strong spiritual allergy to the outside world. If you find that you or a family member struggles to relate to others—for example, feels an aversion to others or a strong wish to keep others at a distance—then resolving that struggle will probably improve your son's condition. Children are very sensitive to the problems that their family struggles with, and these issues can show up on the surface as atopic dermatitis.

Skin problems are usually a manifestation of your rejection of the outside world. So my advice is to practice visualizing a harmonious relationship with others during meditation. If you don't have any relationship problems, try practicing this meditation exercise together with your family members. Of course, more specific treatments may be necessary depending on the condition, but in general, this is often the cause of atopic dermatitis.

HOW TO RAISE AUTISTIC CHILDREN

QUESTION

What are the causes of autism and Asperger syndrome, and how should I raise a child with autism?

ANSWER

Many researchers are classifying, analyzing, and studying various causes of disorders. I have no objection to this scientific research, and I believe that their medical approach may have merit. But one downside may be that a diagnosis can bias our perspective, and we can start seeing everything based on that diagnosis.

If, for example, a doctor tells you that your child is autistic, you may start to define your child in terms of autism and see your child only through the lens of the diagnosis. Or your child may get diagnosed with attention deficit hyperactivity disorder (ADHD) because he is restless. Most children are hyperactive by nature, but once your doctor tells you that your child has ADHD, you might only see him that way. On the contrary, if the doctor simply praised how active your child is, you would see him as a mentally healthy child.

Doctors say that autism is a disorder and not a disease, but they also say that it is an impairment of the growth and development of the brain, which means that it is a physical problem. But this is only speculation. To be quite frank, doctors have no idea what autism really is.

Believing in Your Child's Potential Will Open Up a New Path

There are many different kinds of people in this world, and doctors seem to diagnose children as autistic if they behave in unusual ways, act peculiarly, are troublesome, and keep their parents' and teachers' hands full. But I believe that this definition is too broad. If they were simply saying that these children may have difficulty fitting in with a bureaucratic society or working as an office worker in the corporate world, they might be right. But if we look at people who have become exceptionally successful and made a name for themselves, they are usually quite out of the ordinary.

Those who can do what they are told to do well may be suitable to work as someone's assistant, but people who come up with something completely original and new are usually "weird." Someone even wrote a book about how great men are all strange.* Thomas Edison was eccentric, Ryoma Sakamoto† was unique,

---

* Eiichi Tanizawa, *Erai Hitowa Mina Kawatteharu* ["Great Figures Are All Strange"] (Tokyo: Shinchosha, 2002).
† Ryoma Sakamoto (1836–1867) was a leader of the Meiji Restoration movement, which peacefully restored power to the emperor from the Tokugawa shogunate and ushered in a new era of modernization and prosperity in Japan.

and I myself am different from everyone else.

We shouldn't let social standards decide who we are, and we should not readily accept what doctors say about us or our children. Especially in Japan, those who are different from others and those who have unique personalities are often rejected by society because the Japanese value conformity and the Japanese society expects them to be the same as everybody else. But it is people with strong and unique personalities who change the world, because it takes strength and uniqueness to break through the status quo and bring about unprecedented changes.

Many of the children whom doctors today label as autistic will quite possibly invent extraordinary things and make extraordinary discoveries that will bring about revolutionary changes in the world. And many children diagnosed with ADHD may well grow up to be audacious explorers who travel all around the world.

We should not simply believe that someone has a disorder just because a doctor said so. Doctors are simply labeling these children because they don't know what will become of them. Very often, children with a "disorder" are those with the power to change the world. We should change the existing values that see anyone different as "bad" or "wrong."

If your doctor tells you that your child is autistic, do not let the diagnosis trouble you—instead, believe that your child has a strong and unique personality. Having faith in your child will no doubt open a path to a better future for him or her.

Children Diagnosed with Asperger Syndrome Often Have the Makings of Geniuses and Angels

Asperger syndrome is considered a subtype of autism and is known as a high-functioning disorder. Doctors characterize patients with Asperger syndrome as having extremely high intelligence but lacking the ability to form normal social relationships.

The truth is that these children are actually geniuses. Many child prodigies are different from everyone else. According to the medical definitions, even Albert Einstein would be diagnosed as having Asperger syndrome. It would be absurd to treat such a towering genius only as a patient with a "disorder" and focus on "fixing" him.

Physicians might also label heroes who won't quit until they completely defeat the forces of evil as "patients" suffering from Asperger syndrome, and they might also have assigned this label to religious leaders who brought about religious reforms in the past.

In fact, those with Asperger syndrome often have characteristics of angels of light. When they are born in this world, angels tend to be very meticulous and have a strong sense of justice and fairness and are determined to fight against great forces of evil, all of which makes them look like highly unordinary

 "patients with a disorder" in the eyes of physicians.

So I suggest that you take doctors' words with a grain of salt. You should not take seriously a diagnosis such as "high-functioning disorder," because that diagnosis will

only lead these exceptional people to be ostracized from society, which would be preposterous.

The many different kinds of people in this world simply do not fit into specific definitions or a limited number of classifications. Human beings can transform themselves through the power of faith, so I hope that you will be able to help your child's soul gain that strength.

THE PURPOSE OF CHILDHOOD DISABILITIES

QUESTION

Some children become disabled by illness or accident at an early age of two or three years old. From a spiritual perspective, is this part of their life plan?

ANSWER

Having difficult issues that trouble our mind sometimes causes illness, but some may wonder if this applies to young children, since it seems that two- or three-year-olds could not possibly have complicated issues that torment their minds.

There are general and individual reasons that some young children are struck by serious illness. In general, small children's health conditions reflect the states of the mind of their family members, especially their parents, who are most often closest to them. Young children have not yet developed a sense of self and so are significantly influenced by their parents.

So when children fall ill, it's not the children who have issues that they struggle with, but the parents. The conflict in the parents' mind is most likely causing the children's illness. The parents' negative state of mind gets manifested in the physical condition of their children. Many phenomena arise as manifestations of what goes on in our mind, and children's illnesses are often caused by a troubled mind among their parents and those close to them.

Disabilities Helped Helen Keller Become a Beacon of Hope

Not every individual case, however, is necessarily caused by a parent or family member's issues. There are cases in which there is purpose behind a childhood disability, as exemplified by Helen Keller.

At the age of nineteen months, Helen Keller was struck by an illness that left her blind and deaf. If she had grown up and gone through her life without these disabilities, she would still have been considered a talented woman and a good writer, but she probably would not have inspired and encouraged the world so powerfully.

It was precisely because she triumphed over such harsh handicaps that she became a beacon of hope for many people with disabilities. If someone with no physical disabilities were to tell blind and deaf people to learn contentedness, many of them would probably find it difficult to accept her words. But her words were convincing because she had experienced the difficulty of living with disabilities and had learned how to shine through hardships.

When Criminals Turn Over a New Leaf, They Can Help Others Find Salvation

In a spiritual message, Yuien, a thirteenth-century Buddhist monk and the author of *Tannishou* ("Lamentations of Divergences") said that divine spirits from heaven sometimes purposefully create an adverse situation that gives a villain a chance to turn over a new leaf and straighten himself out, because these incidents have the power to help others get back on the right path.*

Many people may reject the teachings of someone who seems like a born saint or sage. These people would probably feel that pure and good people are like fish living in clean water, but that these fish could never know what it's like to survive in the muddy gutter water. For the purpose of saving these souls, a certain percentage of people who have committed grave crimes go through spiritual regeneration and start walking the right path in life.

One example is Starr Daily, an American gang boss and a hardened criminal in the early 1900s. He made a complete turnaround and started preaching the path to God. He was able to offer hope to those

 who were struggling with their own mistakes and sins; others could see and believe that they, too, could start their lives anew if it was possible for a criminal like him. This is one of the tactics that divine spirits use to guide people.

---

* Ryuho Okawa, *Okawa Ryuho Reigen Zenshuu Dai 17 Kan* ["Ryuho Okawa Spiritual Message Collection Volume 17"] (Tokyo: Happy Science, 2001).

People with Disabilities May Be Meant to Serve as Role Models

If you are not perfectly healthy—for instance, if you have heart disease—it would be easy for you to blame your health problems for your unhappiness. But if you can accomplish great things despite your difficulty, you can become a light of hope and salvation for others. And it is for this purpose of serving as a role model that angels are sometimes born to live with disabilities.

One example is Kiyoshi Yamashita (1922–1951), a genius Japanese artist known for his collages using pieces of colored paper. He is an angel of light who came from the seventh dimension in heaven. He lived with an intellectual disability to encourage others who suffer from handicaps.

Spirits in heaven often feel sorry for angels of light who have to live with an intellectual disability, but these angels are born with the bigger purpose of becoming a role model that others can follow.

In any case, my answer to your question can be summed up in one sentence: Life is a workbook of problems to solve. The child's illness may reflect the state of mind of the child's parents or other close family members and may be part of an effort to teach the parents a lesson. At the same time, great men and women fall ill to show people the many different paths that lead to salvation. If you have any disabilities, I hope that my answer will help you fulfill your purpose and special mission through the way you live.

CURING STUTTERING

QUESTION

I often get stage fright and stutter whenever I have to speak in front of people. Is there any way I can cure myself of stuttering?

ANSWER

Significant numbers of people who stutter are affected spiritually. In fact, in 70 to 80 percent of cases, stuttering is caused by a negative spiritual influence. When someone with a stammer passes away and becomes a negative spirit, the person who falls under his or her influence begins to stutter. Stuttering can be treated in much the same way as we go about removing possessing spirits. We can cure stuttering by cleaning our mind and strengthening the light within.

Developing Expertise Can Help You Overcome a Negative Self-Image

If the stuttering is not caused by spiritual influence, an effective treatment is to overcome it through training and practice. People who stutter tend to be timid and shy, which makes them overreact when they have to stand up and talk in front of people. These people feel a deep sense of inferiority and have a very negative self-image. They feel overwhelmingly ashamed of who they are, so the last thing they want to do is to expose themselves in front of everyone. These people need to conquer these negative feelings to cure their stuttering.

One of the reasons people fear talking in front of people is that they have nothing to talk about. They hide away, thinking that they are not qualified to talk about themselves or share their opinions with others.

One way to overcome these feelings is to find and learn something you can confidently talk about. Acquiring expertise in a certain field will actually make you want to go out and speak to people about it.

Accumulating Experience Is the Best Way to Overcome Fear

Another way to conquer stuttering is to put yourself in the situation that scares you most—speaking in front of people. Fear will come after us as long as we try to run away from it. The more you try to avoid it, the stronger it will become. So you can cure yourself of stuttering by putting yourself in a position where there is no way out but to give a public speech.

This is an extremely effective practice. Even if you feel nervous at first, as you gain a lot of practical experience, you will build up the nerve to speak and will gradually find your mind unwavering. You will become more audacious, which will enable you to speak in front of people without hesitation; you will no longer worry about how others see you. If you can tough it out, you will find that your stuttering is cured.

You feel nervous and stutter because you are overly conscious of what others might think about you, and the best way to overcome this fear is to accumulate a lot of experience. So my advice is to create situations in which you have to stand up and speak in front of people. If you can set your mind to it and take a proactive approach, I'm sure you will be able to cure your stuttering. Where there is a will, there is a way.

TREATING RHEUMATISM

QUESTION

My daughter is suffering from rheumatism and is bedridden throughout most of the day. What causes rheumatism, and what I can do to help her get better?

ANSWER

Rheumatism is almost always caused by spiritual possession. Human spirits that have fallen to the hell of beasts often possess the lower parts of our bodies, but when these spirits constantly cling to us and stay with us all the time, we experience chronic chills in the lower body, making us unable to move our body. These spirits can also attach themselves to our shoulders and necks, causing rheumatism in these parts of the body.

So I'm pretty certain that your daughter's rheumatism is caused by a possessing spirit. And if she is not in a condition to move or practice self-reflection, the only way to cure her is for those around her—her family members—to seek right mind and strengthen their inner light. Doing this will remove the possessing spirit from your daughter's body.

In a sense, it is easy to heal an illness that's caused by a possessing spirit, because it will heal completely once the spirit is expelled. Exorcising the spirit will be 100 percent effective.

Creating a Harmonious, Loving, and Happy Family Can Be the Remedy for Rheumatism

As her parent, I'm sure you can tell, at least to some degree, what the cause of her rheumatism might be. When you examine your daughter's life in light of the teachings of the Truths, do you find anything that she has done wrong? If not, I would like you to ponder whether anyone close to her, such as a family member, could be exerting a negative influence on her.

Some people are spiritually sensitive and can keenly sense when spirits are near them. These people can be vulnerable to the evil spirits that are possessing people close to them; even if they themselves haven't done anything particularly bad to attract such spirits, they can easily be affected by them. Evil spirits always go after the easiest prey, the member of the family who is most vulnerable to spiritual possession.

Examine whether your daughter has had any problems that might have triggered spiritual possession. If you don't find anything, then ponder whether anyone else in the family might be taking the wrong path in life. If so, then that person needs to repent and change his or her thoughts and actions. If that person is incapable of practicing self-reflection, then other family members should provide an example to follow. They should strengthen their inner light and create a harmonious, loving, and happy family. The last thing you want for your daughter is a cold, distant, and harsh family atmosphere.

If you take courage, increase the inner light of those around her, and earnestly wish to heal her illness, I have complete faith that she will recover.

THE SPIRITUAL TRUTH BEHIND INCURABLE DISEASES

QUESTION

As a medical student in clinical training, I treat young patients who are suffering from leukemia and other incurable diseases. What are the causes of incurable diseases, and what is the spiritual meaning and purpose of such diseases?

ANSWER

Leukemia and other blood-related diseases clearly have spiritual causes. Blood carries the very source of life and nourishes the entire body. What this means is that those who develop a blood disease are usually affected by spiritual factors that prevent them from living a life of growth and prosperity.

Cause #1: Karma from a Past Life

Two types of spiritual factors affect our well-being. The first is the karma that is deeply embedded within our soul even before we are born into this world (see the inset "Life Is Like a Workbook" in part I, chapter 2). Unfortunately, those who inflicted harm on others in a past life often have the karma to develop a blood-related illness in this life. To be more specific, memories of having seen blood or of being responsible for other people's deaths are deeply engraved in their soul.

If they can completely make amends for their sins after they return to the other world in the afterlife, they won't have to carry them over into their next incarnation. But usually that's not the case, and many of these souls are reborn with a plan to resolve their karma so that they can make complete amends for their mistakes before they finish this lifetime.

When these souls are born into this world, their karma often manifests as blood-related ailments. Some of them may not develop an illness during childhood but gradually develop one later in life. These souls have a predisposition for self-destruction. Their experience of spilling blood in a past life creates a self-tormenting mentality that often gives rise to a pathology.

Our physical bodies are not created spontaneously; it is actually the mind, the core part of our soul, that constructs and maintains the body. Those who subconsciously hold self-punishing thoughts often become ill. In a sense, these people are predestined to develop a blood-related disease.

Cause #2: Negative Spiritual Influences

Another factor that triggers an incurable disease is the influence of evil spirits. When spiritual possession occurs, the possessed person develops symptoms of the same disease that caused the death of the possessing spirit. For example, if we are possessed by the wandering spirit of someone who suffered the after-effects of atomic bombing and died of a blood-related illness, we will develop the symptoms of that disease.

Although our bodies have the ability to eliminate harmful substances, when we are under negative spiritual influence, our power to fight against these substances becomes weak, letting them take root and spread in our body.

In fact, most pathological phenomena that afflict the body occur this way. The human mind has the power to materialize its thoughts. And a negative thought, when it has a specific target, manifests itself and becomes a physical ailment.

As I said earlier, although the plague and cholera subsided, they reappeared in the form of new diseases such as AIDS (see the inset "What Causes Viruses to Spread?" in part II, chapter 3). Similarly, until we eliminate the root cause of an ailment, even if we treat it with medication or prevent it from becoming symptomatic, it will find a way to reemerge as a different physical disease and keep coming back in a seemingly endless cycle.

Fish Skin Disease Is Caused by the Animosity of Creatures Who Died from Pollution

Among the large number of rare and incurable diseases today, many are fairly new. Oddly enough, the number of dermatological diseases is on the rise. This increase has been caused by the many creatures that have been driven out of their natural habitats and had their ecosystems, especially the oceans and rivers, destroyed by urban development and pollution.

All creatures, including fish and animals, basically possess the same capacity for joy, anger, sorrow, and pleasure as we humans do. And naturally, they have a sense of happiness and unhappiness, as well. When coastal and river pollution lead a great number of creatures to suffer and die, they collectively harbor feelings of anger and resentment for having their lives taken en masse for no apparent reason.

People living near industrial areas built on coasts and along rivers develop fish skin disease, which makes the skin scaly, rough, and thick like that of a fish. This disease can almost never be cured by medical treatment, because it is caused by the collective sentiment of the spirits that died from pollution.

Muscle Atrophy Is Caused by Karma or Spiritual Possession

Muscle atrophy is another incurable disease that has spiritual causes. This disease has two basic causes. The first is karma from a past life. What kind of karma do you think someone whose muscles gradually waste away has? As you may have guessed, this disease is a reaction to their involvement in restricting others' bodily freedom.

Readings of those who have been diagnosed with muscle atrophy would indeed show that many of them had crippled others in past lives. For example, during war, they would take prisoners of war into custody and force them into hard labor or inflict corporal punishment. These people develop muscle atrophy or become physically disabled as the karma of their previous reincarnation. This is one cause of muscle diseases.

Another cause is negative spiritual influence. Animal spirits are often the culprits of muscle atrophy; the patient develops symptoms when these spirits possess their arms and legs.

Physical Hardship May Be Part of a Life Plan

Of course, not everyone's illness can be attributed to karma. Some people develop a disease as a way to do the work of angels. As I mentioned earlier, Helen Keller chose to live with disabilities so that she could fulfill a higher purpose. Similarly, Stephen Hawking, the world-famous genius physicist with a muscle-related disease called amyotrophic lateral sclerosis (ALS), entered this world with the purpose of educating others through his disability.

Some people become socially active despite being confined to a wheelchair. These people may feel that it's unfair that they have to live with a disability, but some of them did plan their life that way, daring to take on the challenge. They chose to live with a physical handicap to inspire others with courage, joy, and a sense of life's purpose.

From a spiritual perspective, our life in this world is only temporary, so some people take on a difficult challenge to gain virtue through their hardships. When they return to the other world, they will be cured of all physical disabilities and regain the freedom that they once had.

Filling Your Mind with Positive Thoughts Can Improve Your Physical Condition

While I cannot cover every single case, people with incurable or rare diseases can be classified into the three general groups that I have outlined here: those who develop an illness because of karma from a past life, those who are affected by negative spiritual influence, and those who chose to live with a disease to fulfill their mission. Among these three types, most people fall into the first or the second one based on the principle of self-responsibility.

People in the second group—those who are affected by evil spirits—have issues in their mind that attract these spirits. As I have explained many times in my books, it is a spiritual law that those with the same mental wavelengths attract one another. So we are spiritually connected to whatever world is inhabited by spirits whose vibrations are similar to ours. This means that our mind is what attracts negative vibrations—although the problems that we struggle with vary greatly depending on the individual.

In some cases, the cause of the negative spiritual influence may be not our own issues but rather the troubles and problems of our family members. We are still responsible for it, however, because we let it get to us. To dispel the spiritual influence, we need to completely change the wavelengths of our mind so that it will no longer be in tune with the negative vibrations of evil spirits.

The wavelength we want to tune our mind to is that of divine spirits. To be on the same wavelength as the divine spirits, we need to fill our mind with bright and positive thoughts, hope, love, and courage. Abandon all your negative thoughts, turn your mind toward a positive direction, and start thinking positively and constructively.

Even if you have a family member who is suffering from a disease, you can still brighten up your home by  making an effort to live with positive and happy thoughts. About 70 to 80 percent of diseases are caused by our state of mind. If we are ill, it is important to know that our mind is often inviting the illness and that healing our mind is the first step to curing it.

7

ENCOURAGEMENT FOR PEOPLE WHO HAVE LOST THEIR EYESIGHT

QUESTION

I have lost my eyesight. What sort of attitude should I take as I make my way through life?

ANSWER

Each of us goes through pain and sufferings in life. You may be suffering from an issue that I don't have, which may make you envy my life, but I also have my own problems that I struggle with.

Sometimes, you may feel as though you are the only one carrying your cross while everyone else is happy and has nothing troubling their mind. We are prone to blame our unhappiness on disadvantages that others don't have, and we think that we could be happy just like everyone else *if only* we could remove that flaw.

Suffering Can Be the Key to Understanding Your Life Purpose

My advice is not to think of whatever makes you different from others—your environment, personality, physical characteristics, or ability—as a cause of your suffering that you need to escape from. Instead, try to see it as the key to solving the problems in the workbook of your life. This is an important point to bear in mind.

Your vision impairment is material for your soul's growth. You might not be able to completely understand its significance in this lifetime alone, but by living with a disability, I'm sure you feel very keenly how happy you would be if you could have your vision back. As the saying goes, "It is not until we lose our health that we recognize its blessing." We often do not know how blessed we are for being born with no physical disabilities and for having eyesight and hearing.

Many people today are physically challenged. Some have paralyzed legs, others have no arms, and still others are blind or deaf. Some of these people have karma from their past lives that caused their disability in their present incarnation. In your case, you lost your eyesight because it was necessary for your soul to appreciate the blessing of being able to see.

We Are All Given a Specific Workbook of Life for Our Soul Growth

If I conduct spiritual readings on someone, I can go back in time to see what happened to that person in many past lives during the last five thousand to ten thousand years, but going through the life history of each individual would be an endless task.

No matter what happened in our past lives, we should tackle the issues in the workbook given to us in this lifetime and strive to find an answer to each of the problems. We are all given different workbooks, because they are made specifically for each of us to help our soul grow. So instead of trying to run away from the problems we face or refusing to solve them, we should all seek the purpose behind our problems.

Your challenge is to find a way to live a life full of light in spite of your vision impairment. Your life is a success if, through the way you live it, you can inspire and ignite high aspirations even in those who have good eyesight.

Live the Best Life You Can in the Circumstances You're In

All physical disabilities will be cured once you return to the other world. You will regain your eyesight, and others will regain their hearing. Your physical disability will only last for several decades in this world, which is a short period of time in the eternal cycle of reincarnation.

The role you're playing in this life is a part of your ongoing spiritual training. So instead of believing that you will be happy if you can cure your physical disability, turn your attention to how to live the best life you possibly can within the circumstances you are in now. You

may feel bad about asking others for
help and support, but I'm sure there
are things you can give in return.
The important thing is not to think
negatively, but to focus on the positive in everything you do.

Even if you cannot see with your physical eyes, you
can still see with your spiritual eyes. So discover the
Truths with your inner sight, and create something
positive using your mouth and ears.

This is all part of the workbook assigned specifically
to you, so try to solve the problems in this lifetime.
You will be given the answers to the problems in
your workbook when you return to the other world.
You will know then why you went through the spiritual
training that you are now undergoing. Until that day,
I hope that you will keep working hard to solve the
problems that have been given to you.

Continued Spiritual Study and Practice Can Extend Your Life

It seems that continued practice of intense study and deep contemplation for decades leads to longevity, as is the case for many religious seekers. Conversely, when religious practitioners start slacking in their studies and spiritual discipline, they run out of things to teach, and that usually marks the end of their life.

For example, the thirteenth-century Japanese Buddhist monk Shinran maintained a strong intellectual capacity even at the age of ninety. His complete devotion to two decades of study when he was younger built the intellectual foundation that kept him going strong until his nineties. Followers of Shin Buddhism, the sect founded by Shinran, often deny the necessity of studying the teachings or reciting the sutras, but Shinran himself was a very studious practitioner who pursued intense study of Buddhist teachings on Mt. Hiei.

Theologians and other religious scholars who studied Buddhism and Indian philosophy and passed away at seventy or eighty years old are often said to have died "prematurely." Scholars of Eastern philosophy lament the passing of an eighty-year-old man, saying that he was "still so young," because these scholars usually live well into their nineties. One reason for their longevity is that there is so much to study. There are so many scriptures in Buddhism that it takes forever to study the complete Buddhist canon.

The founder of Buddhism, Shakyamuni Buddha, offered a wide range of teachings—in fact, the total number amounts to as many as eighty-four thousand. Of course, expounding that many teachings takes a long time, which is why Shakyamuni Buddha had to live to old age. In contrast, Jesus Christ taught passionately and fervently, which probably made it difficult for him to continue preaching for a long period of time and led to his early death.

Another reason that studying Buddhist teachings leads us to longevity is that it gives us peace of mind. Leading an orderly life based on the practice of Buddhist teachings, for example by reciting sutras every day, naturally helps us develop tolerance. We become peaceful, patient, and tranquil, which will allow us to live up to ninety years or more.

Like Buddhism, my organization Happy Science offers a large volume of teachings, which is good news because this means that studying our teachings can help many people live long lives.

CHAPTER 5

MINDSETS FOR CAREGIVERS AND HEALTHCARE PROFESSIONALS

THE POWER OF A POSITIVE MINDSET

QUESTION

I take care of many patients who are struggling through not only a physical illness, but also fears and anxieties about their condition. What are some things that I can do to help them cope with their inner suffering?

ANSWER

Being a physician or healthcare professional gives you many opportunities to offer words of comfort to those who are struggling with illnesses. The things you say to your patients can make a big difference in the way you make them feel about their illness, and I'm certain that it is worth looking into this to see if you can improve the quality of the things you say to patients. Many doctors who feel the weight of their responsibility tend to explain the worst possible scenarios that their patients' conditions can lead to. They do this out of fear that a patient they diagnose as curable may die after all.

Since the responsibility for these mistakes mostly falls on the doctors, doctors have become accustomed to adopting a pessimistic outlook. For example, doctors often tell their patients that a surgical operation has a fifty-fifty success rate or warn them that the operation will not guarantee their life but then say that they will do their best if the patient still wants to proceed with the operation. Since there are bound to be some positive diagnoses that take a turn for the worse, many doctors have built up a pessimistic mindset as they have run into these experiences over the course of their career.

Positive Words Help Promote the Healing Process

But because of the powerful impact that words have on the human mind, healthcare professionals are in a blessed position to help their patients by giving them positive messages of hope. Healing and longevity will seem like lost causes to a patient who receives a diagnosis of terminal illness. And if, on top of that, other members of the family are also persuaded of an imminent death, with perhaps three months remaining at best, then a sense of hopelessness will weigh down everyone's hearts and do little to improve the patient's chances for healing, and it may even contribute to the patient's eventual death. On the other hand, many people have found healing through positive words that salved their sunken spirits and restored vital energy and a healthful flush to their flesh.

Adopting a positive mindset alone can help turn around the health of many of your patients. You can begin by finding a deeper awareness of the power of your words to bring hope or despair to people's hearts.

Have confidence that your positive mindset and positive words can only improve your patients' health.

Since I am keenly aware of the impact of my words on people's spirits, if a hospital ever hires me to spend some time with their patients, many patients will quickly find that they've healed and no longer need to stay in the hospital. I don't have any medical experience or training, but I am certain that many patients will notice a dramatic improvement in their health just by letting me have a conversation with them.

Fostering Your Patients' Natural Healing Ability

What this all means is that we human beings are not just material objects. We are really spiritual creatures with a mind that holds tremendous influence over the condition of our body. Even if an illness afflicts our physical body, we can heal that illness by thinking thoughts of vital, life-giving energy.

When we look into the mind of an ill person, we see that it is greatly distressed by negative thoughts and feelings. The person may suffer from grievances, dissatisfaction, envy, spite, resentment, blame of others, and blame of circumstances. These mindsets oppose the light of the Truths and exacerbate the person's illness. We were born with a powerful ability to heal our bodies, but instead of harnessing this power, we often allow pessimistic beliefs to manifest illness and interfere with healing.

Helping an ill person shift away from these negative mindsets will dramatically improve their health. Healthcare professionals can help their patients by encouraging them to make positive changes to their thoughts and to believe in their power to bring healing upon themselves.

TAKING CARE OF A PARENT WITH DEMENTIA

QUESTION

My mother, who will soon be turning eighty-two, has been diagnosed with senile dementia. Could you offer me advice for the struggles we may face together as her condition progresses over time?

ANSWER

It's not a surprise for someone of your mother's age to be showing signs of senile dementia. Since senile dementia will not hamper your mother's passage to heaven, you don't have to be worried for her where-abouts in the afterlife. What you see in her symptoms are only the degenerative effects of aging on her brain, which create a dissonance between what she—her soul—wishes for her body to do and her body's actual ability or inability to do so.

My Father's Message from Heaven Proved that His Soul Was Healthy

My father also suffered some impairment before his passing at the age of eighty-two. It was some seven months before his death that we discovered a tumor in his brain and saw some visible signs of impairment to his cognitive functions. But shortly after his death, he was able to immediately get to work again in heaven. He promptly set out to compose haiku verses to set his thoughts and messages into poems, and then he brought them to me in spirit within one or two days of his passing.* This tells us that the decline of the brain and the consequent loss of bodily control did not damage his soul. His soul continued to live in perfect health, despite the outward signs we saw of his physical decline.

The appearance of my father's spirit also began to change, as if to turn back time. Within one or two months, he resembled the way he had looked at the age of sixty-five. And the clock seemed only to know how to run backwards, because his youthful transformation took him as far back as his forties. I saw clearly that there was nothing ailing his soul; his soul remained in perfect condition.

Just as my father's soul was healthful and full of vitality in the afterlife in heaven, you need not have concerns about problems your mother may have in the other world.

---

* Ryuho Okawa, *Spiritual Message from Saburo Yoshikawa: Sermon From the Afterlife Volume 1* (Tokyo: Happy Science, 2001).

The Pain of This World Adds to the Bliss of the Other World

Your mother may face some hard moments as she nears death. But the pain of these moments will only add to the bliss of liberation on her journey, enlarging the happiness and delight she will feel as she finds her way to the afterlife.

As her caregiver, you will probably find your mother often wanting to express grievances to you. As her legs become less agile and mobile, she'll feel frustrated and fearful of becoming confined to bed. If she is suffering from cancer, she will anguish in her pain. Each time her memory fails her, she will roil in exasperation. And she will rankle in her hurt pride when she feels she's being treated as if she were crazy, when she can find nothing wrong with herself. As caregivers, we need to embrace these moments as the natural signs of decline, a rite of passage that also awaits each of us in the autumn of our life.

When you and your mother find yourselves struggling during this difficult time together, rest your thoughts on the day when your mother will pass on to the bliss of heaven. In heaven, your mother will savor the joy of a cicada that lifts into freedom out of the shackles of its heavy shell. Rest assured that those who are bound for heaven will find happiness—though this won't hold true for those who are bound elsewhere—for hell.

If your mother is suffering from senile dementia now, you and your family must be feeling the weight of this burden. And your mother, knowing the encumbrances that must be falling on you and your family, is surely feeling remorseful and wishing within her heart that she could tell you how sorry she is. This is as much a time of hardship to her family as it is to her. But every ounce of hardship endured will hardly go to waste; it is rendered for the sake of the greater happiness she will reap in the other world.

Caregiving Is a Chance to Practice Giving Love

The burden that has fallen on you and her family may be the chance you've been given to repay her for all she's done for you since your childhood. It may be that it's a part of your duty as her child. It may also mean that you may find yourself in the same circumstances come the autumn of your own life in this world. Whatever purpose this hardship is meant to bring to your life, this is a blessed chance to practice giving love. To be by her side patiently through this ordeal with a heart of fortitude is a true mark of your love.

What I have said about senile dementia is also true for Alzheimer's disease. Alzheimer's disease is not the sign of a life spent in wrong deeds. Rather, it is a manifestation of the "mechanical" decline of aging from which our bodies, including the cognitive functions, cannot escape. But whatever signs of physical weakening we may develop in the twilight of our lives, they will not impact our spiritual existence itself. Spiritually, our souls will continue to live and think healthfully. Even if we suffer from Alzheimer's disease, the soul that lives within is fully vital and conscious of much that happens around it, including the gripes and grievances that slip from people's utterances. So, if we have an elderly family member struggling with

Alzheimer's disease, we need to be conscious and mindful that his or her soul is hearing and understanding the things we say.

The day of your mother's departure to heaven is probably already set. So the remainder of her time in this world has been given to you as a precious opportunity to give your all to the practice of giving love. I hope you'll rest assured that the signs of your mother's decline won't pose any hindrances to her eventual passage to heaven.

TAKING CARE OF A BEDRIDDEN PARENT AT HOME

QUESTION

My mother-in-law became very ill a year ago and has been bedridden ever since. It has been challenging and difficult to take care of her while I manage household responsibilities as I also raise my child. I often feel overcome with everything that I'm shouldering and have come to a point of physical and mental exhaustion. Could you offer me spiritual guidance for finding my way through these feelings of exhaustion and despair?

ANSWER

From a broad view of human life in this world, we can say that almost every household will someday have to face the challenge of caring for an ailing or disabled loved one at home. Having someone you care about fall victim to an illness, an injury, or a tragic disaster, and then facing the prospect of ensuing death—these are life-shattering moments found dotted along the course of many of our lives that no one can completely escape from. These are hard experiences that can bring the strongest of hearts to the abyss of grief and despair. It can be a challenge not to let negative feelings shake our hearts when we have someone suffering from an illness or tragedy to whose care we need to devote everything we have.

My advice is to take the negative outlook of such circumstances with a grain of salt and instead to look to the bright side, the positive purpose that every tragedy of life is meant to teach us. We human beings are essentially spiritual beings with souls. But, for the span of some decades, we decided to assume physical bodies. We decided to do so because this world offers precious experiences to foster the spiritual growth of our souls. Without our bodies, we wouldn't be able to go through these ordeals—such as the physical pain and discomfort of an illness.

But when we go through these physical ordeals, our spiritual essence within remains unscathed and whole. Our souls restore themselves to vitality when we resume our original life in the other world.

The suffering your mother is now going through is not meant to be eternal suffering. This suffering is just a part of her soul's temporary growing experience in this world. Her illness may seem tragic and torturous to you right now. But there is an afterlife in heaven, where a life of perfect health and freedom awaits her when she is relieved of her physical existence.

If this is the truth of human life, then whatever suffering transpires in your future—whether her condition progresses or her body succumbs to the illness—it's far more important for you and her alike to see your lives and circumstances from the perspective of the other world. The life we live in this world is really a time of preparation, a time of rehearsal, for the real life that is in store for us in the other world. So we must cherish our time here as a chance to learn the lessons within each problem, each crisis, and each event in this life and turn them into positive, growing experiences for our soul. Doing this is the effort that is desired of everyone—both givers and receivers of love—by the existence that has placed us in this system.

Turning Tragedy and Sorrow into Polishing Stones for Your Soul

What I say is not meant to be severe or to further discourage you as you struggle with this challenge. But it is certain your ordeal has a purpose: to make your soul shine brighter by encouraging you to find the resolute cheer, positive mindset, and passionate hope that you need to stand up to these adverse circumstances. When we humans accept that every moment of suffering and sorrow that comes our way is a polishing stone to help make our soul shine brighter, we can endure any kind of suffering or sorrow.

There have been many times in the lives of others when ordeals like yours brought about an inner spiritual leap toward faith. It is in these times of deep grief and sorrow that we humans seek to be saved and discover that the key to salvation lies within the depths of our souls. Therefore, you need not view your circumstance as a reason for unhappiness. Your circumstance is really a precious opportunity for your soul to grow. This is a priceless treasure to be thankful for. This experience is your chance to polish and elevate the spirituality of your heart and soul.

Illness Brings Fortitude to Your Love

Caring for an ill family member lets us learn a lot about what it means to give our love, give of ourselves, and serve others. This gives us a chance to cultivate a sense of selfless devotion, which we cannot give unless we also have fortitude and acceptance.

We often find it to be easy to love someone, such as our spouse, when their life is going well and they stay youthful and attractive. But what will happen when your spouse faces unemployment or when beauty and attractiveness fade? Will your willingness to be giving remain steady and unchanged? Even our willingness to give love to our spouse can be strained when we go through changes that are beyond our control. The practice of fortitude and acceptance is essential to our love for this reason. Fortitude and acceptance are there to help us when obstacles make it challenging to give of our love. Similarly, we need to be patient and strong when a loved one in the family falls ill, and this is especially true because we share so much of our lives with our family members.

Those who are afflicted with illness are also being given a chance to reflect on their attitude toward their circumstance. This is a time when they are allowed to realize that they now require the love and support of others. They need to accept this circumstance, dissolve whatever resentment or frustration they may feel for this fate, and resolve to bring peace and calm to their hearts as soon as they can so as to bring some relief and joy to those around them. It's time for them to let go of resentment, seek inner repose, and give everything they have to healing and renewal.

Sometimes, their search for healing may still lead them to their death. But wherever fate takes them, their perseverance in maintaining a positive attitude in the midst of struggle will not be in vain. When they cast off their physical garb, they will be led to the bright world of heaven. When we cast away resentment and choose to accept everything that comes our way as spiritual nourishment for our soul, we will find the light of true happiness shining forth.

Preventing Heart Disease

Cardiovascular disease is the number one cause of death worldwide. Most cases of this disease are caused by lifestyle-related issues such as a high consumption of fats, high-calorie diets, and a lack of exercise. So while some diseases are brought about by spiritual influences caused by distresses within the mind, the primary causes of heart-related diseases are problems with our physical condition. We can easily determine who has a high risk of heart disease by looking at people's lifestyle habits.

If, when you review your day-to-day activities and lifestyle habits, you feel that you could be at risk for a fatal heart-related illness down the road, it's very important to your health and well-being that you garner your willpower and resolve to change them. A healthy diet includes fats and calories, but they should be in moderate amounts, and if you are consuming more than what's considered healthy, then you should consider cutting back on how much of these you eat each day.

One of the common pitfalls many people are prone to overlook is the high calorie content of alcoholic beverages. It's easy to dismiss the health risks posed by beverages if we're not accustomed to thinking of drinks as having a lot of calories. But if you go out to a bar to drink and snack with your friends and then also have a small dinner at home, you can easily rack up three or four thousand calories worth of food and drink for the entire day, and that is a sure recipe for disaster down the line.

You can successfully prevent heart disease just by improving your lifestyle habits. I highly recommend that you start to follow a health-conscious lifestyle early on, in your thirties, because physical decline often begins at that age. By incorporating proper amounts of exercise, eating a nutritious diet, learning how to maintain a healthy weight, and getting enough rest, you will be able to successfully prevent heart disease.

Conscious Breathing Can Remove Negative Spiritual Influences

Body parts with blood congestion or accumulated fatigue often become targets of spiritual possession. Areas that often get stiff or tense, such as the back of the head, the neck and shoulders, and the lower back, can be especially vulnerable to attack by negative spiritual influences.

Common signs of spiritual possession include extreme fatigue, heaviness, stiffness, and pain in the neck or other body parts after going out into town or to a crowded place. Those who habitually experience this pattern of symptoms first need to regulate the rhythms of their bodies to remove possessing spirits.

To tune up your system and adjust your body flow, focus on your breathing. As you take in fresh oxygen, visualize your blood circulating slowly throughout your entire body, from your head through your neck and shoulders to your waist and all your body parts, without disruption. This breathing exercise will allow you to remove the discordant vibrations from your body.

When you feel extremely exhausted, it is often a sign of your blood thickening and clotting. Light aerobic exercise will improve your blood circulation, which will make it easier for you to receive God's light. You can then gradually relax your body, regulate your breathing, and gain peace of mind.

Part III

Healing Yourself with
the Power of Faith

YOUR BODY REFLECTS YOUR SELF-IMAGE

Your Body Is Constantly Renewing Itself

We human beings are born in a body that weighs about seven pounds or so, but after several decades, absolutely no part of that physical body that came out of the womb remains with us.

The true nature of the physical body is like a flowing stream. Every cell in our body is eventually replaced by a new cell; our bones, organs, and even our skulls are completely renewed with the passing of time. The bodies we have today are not only completely different from the ones we were born in, but are also constantly changing even now. New cells replace old cells every day, and a large part of the body gets replaced over the course of a month. Over the past year, your body has been almost completely renewed.

Some people say that they were born with frail health or that their genes predispose them to certain diseases. But if your health has been bad since you were born, even though your body is constantly changing, it only means that you have continued to reproduce your bad health over and over again.

The Mind Can Both Cause and Heal Illness

What maintains our physical self is a picture we hold in our mind; our self-image is the blueprint of our body. If we continue to hold negative thoughts or ill will toward ourselves, telling ourselves, for example, that we are sick and unhappy and that we will be pitied by others and die soon, these thoughts will manifest themselves and become reality.

We have a spiritual body, known as the "astral body," which is the outermost part of the spiritual body and an exact representation of the physical body. The astral body is made up of multiple layers of spiritual bodies and receives the signals and messages that our mind transmits. When our negative thoughts distort our astral body, they manifest as physical ailments. In fact, most illnesses are caused by our own mind.

This negative effect can occur in the opposite direction as well. When the physical body is damaged, it hurts the astral body and negatively affects the spiritual body, which further damages our physical condition, thereby creating a vicious cycle of worsening well-being.

Buddhism teaches that the body and the mind are not separable, but are one. They are perfectly integrated. But ultimately, it is our mind that creates our physical body, so the image we hold in our mind affects the condition of our astral body, determining how healthy or unhealthy our physical body becomes.

This perspective helps us become aware of our enormous potential to heal ourselves. You may be fighting a disease now, or you may fall ill in the future, or you may have been battling illness for a long time. Whatever the case, realizing that the body you have now is entirely different from the body you were born in and that your mind has been creating your physical body is the key to good health.

YOUR MIND DETERMINES YOUR HEALTH

Your Unconscious Controls Your Well-Being

While we can consciously control some of our body functions —for example, we can move our muscle to raise our arm— most parts of our body function unconsciously. Blood circulates throughout our body without our intention or effort. Our heart keeps beating whether or not we want it to. We also breathe quite naturally and automatically. Although we can consciously regulate our breathing, we are not always aware that we are constantly breathing throughout the day. In this way, many of our body parts and cells operate automatically. In fact, the unconscious controls most regions of the body.

The human body houses a multitude of cells, as numerous as the stars in the sky. Trillions of microorganisms reside inside our body. And from the standpoint of each cell and the microbes inside the body, our internal organs are as vast as the galaxy.

Our unconscious mind exerts a great amount of influence over our health. In fact, our physical well-being depends much more on the regions of the body controlled by the unconscious than on those we control consciously.

Self-Destructive Thoughts Create Harmful Cells

So it is our unconscious that has the power to create disease. The negative thoughts we hold on a conscious level penetrate deep into the unconscious mind like sediment and often become the seeds of disease. These malignant thoughts manifest in the physical body as illnesses such as cancer and other disorders of internal organs. Many diseases in the liver, heart, lungs, kidneys, blood vessels, and brain are often the products of negative thoughts that we have held over the years and that have infiltrated our unconscious mind.

Painful experiences of mistreatment, abuse, or discrimination can give rise to negative feelings of hatred and anger. When these bottled-up emotions pile up inside, they often become the mental seat of the disease and produce self-destructive cells in the body. Almost all cases of cancer are caused by harmful cells within our body. These cells are nurtured by self-destructive thoughts—most often thoughts of hatred or fear.

But the fact that we create cells that harm us means that we also have the power to cure ourselves. And we can harness this healing power by holding thoughts that are the complete opposite of destructive and negative thoughts.

Our unconscious has the power to build or destroy our physical body. Knowing this is crucial to protecting ourselves from illness.

USING THE POWER OF FAITH TO FIGHT DISEASE

Removing Negative Thoughts Is Crucial to Curing Disease

Those who develop cancer often find within themselves aggressive emotions toward others, such as hatred, anger, envy, and jealousy, and negative thoughts about others, such as grudges and abusive words. These thoughts and feelings, when harbored for a long period of time, pile up inside the mind and trigger the development of cancer. To prevent cancer, it is crucial that we clean our mind of these negative thoughts that have accumulated over the years. We can do this by reflecting on our thoughts and actions or seeking the guidance of someone who has gained a high level of awareness.

In a Japanese animation movie called *Spirited Away* there is a scene in which the heroine uses warm water to clean the smelly spirit of a polluted river whose entire body is soaked in gooey sludge. The movie's director must have an affinity with the minor realm of the spirit world to be able to depict such mysterious creatures. Spiritually, those whose minds are full of dark and negative thoughts look like this river spirit, covered in viscous and muddy sludge.

It's only a matter of course that people with such dark, sticky, and smudgy minds develop illness. They could also attract negativity and misfortunes such as traffic accidents in their family. Removing these muddy, negative thoughts from the mind is crucial to our ability to heal ourselves.

At Happy Science, we offer ritual prayers to help cure various illnesses, but first and foremost, we all need to become aware that we already have the power to heal ourselves. We can all cure ourselves and improve our lives by learning the right laws of the mind, turning our minds toward the bright world of heaven, and starting to walk down the right path.

Faith Can Boost Our Immunity

Recent research in medical science has begun to discover the relationship between a weakened immune system and the development of diseases. A deteriorated immune system can let viruses, infections, and germs enter our body, causing illness and, in the worst cases, death.

We can boost our immunity, however, by using the power of faith, or our ability to believe. In other words, we can use the power of our mind—our willpower. Our earnest wish to serve God as a living angel will fill our entire body with a dynamic and positive energy that will eventually spread into every cell in all parts of our body and improve our immunity.

Boosting our immunity this way can even cure early-stage cancer. Not only can we combat cancer this way, we can also share the power of our faith with others to improve their immune systems. We can help them foster zest for life in each of their body cells by enthusiastically guiding them to the right path and thereby brightening up their hearts.

When we are determined to conquer illness so that we can accomplish a greater mission in life, our aspiration will spread to each of our cells and fill our entire body with a surge of power from within. By firmly believing in our purpose, we will find rejuvenating power welling up from within, making us feel ten or twenty years younger.

ARE YOU IN LOVE WITH ILLNESS?

The Root Cause of Illness May Be Your Underlying Wish to Become Sick

While we cannot completely avoid all illness as we go through life, in many instances, we become sick because our inner self is seeking illness. A sick person would probably be offended if he were told that he fell ill because he likes being sick, but in fact, many people fall ill because of their affinity for illness. There are numerous cases in which people who have failed in relationships or in their business find no other escape but to seek asylum in disease. They push themselves to become sick, believing that illness will redeem them from their failure or mistakes and release them from their responsibility.

This doesn't necessarily happen consciously; we can unconsciously invite illnesses. Our underlying wish to fall sick may drive us to lead an unhealthy lifestyle or take part in extreme activities that take a toll on our body, pushing ourselves to the limit until we collapse. Unaware of our unconscious wish, we may come to believe that we are unfortunate victims of fate.

When we become sick, others might feel sorry for us and care for us, which may comfort us. But we should know that the root cause of illness is the wish to become ill, which often springs from a desire to run away from a difficult problem we are struggling with.

The Vision in Your Mind Creates Your Future Self

If we really wish to be successful, we should be mindful of our health. When we recognize the early signs of illnesses, we should take caution and seek the advice of family and friends. And based on their suggestions, we should change any work habits or lifestyle practices that may endanger our health.

But those who are in love with illness never listen to others' advice. Even if people around them warn them for months before that they will collapse if they continue their current lifestyle, they nevertheless keep going and then suddenly fall ill. The cause of illness in this case is their irresponsibility.

If we truly feel responsible for our work, we will realize ahead of time that our falling sick will cause problems not only for ourselves but for others as well. So we will take precautions to prevent health problems. But those who lack a sense of responsibility often ignore these warning signs, push themselves to the limit, and end up causing trouble for everyone else.

In short, our health hinges on our vision of what we want to become deep within: a happy and successful person or an unhappy failure.

5

USING PRAYER TO RECHARGE YOUR SPIRITUAL ENERGY

Prayer Can Help You Receive Light from Heaven

We can use prayer to recharge our spiritual energy. Sit quietly and pray to God for inexhaustible energy, infinite wisdom, and unlimited love. In your prayer, visualize yourself receiving wonderful energy pouring down from heaven.

Picture God's unlimited love flowing into you. When your entire body feels filled with God's love, ponder how you can share this love with everyone in the world.

You can also imagine God's unlimited power flowing into you, giving you boundless strength. When you feel fully recharged with God's power, contemplate how you can use this infinite power to move forward in life and contribute to the world.

I practice this prayer regularly. I work every day, but some days I feel under the weather or exhausted. On those days, I practice this prayer to receive light from divine spirits in heaven. I can receive heaven's light on my own, but I often ask one of the divine spirits to recharge my energy. As the light enters my body and fills me up, it empowers me to get to my next task.

This prayer can easily be answered; many divine spirits have no problem granting our wish to receive light from heaven. What's important is that we cultivate a compassionate heart to using the light that we've received for the improvement of the world.

6

EL CANTARE HEALING: A PRAYER FOR HEALING ILLNESSES

Nothing Is Impossible for the Creator

Illness is a product of our thoughts; it arises from a disharmony between the mind and the body. There is nothing that humans have created that God cannot erase, because God is omnipotent and almighty. God created the universe, the sun, the stars, the flora, fauna of the Earth, and human beings all by His will. Because God is the creator of all things—all of us are manifestations of God's light—there is nothing that God cannot eliminate in this world, not least a tiny lesion in our body.

God has the power to let this entire planet vanish or appear in the blink of an eye. Although He has absolute power over all creation, God has temporarily entrusted human beings to govern this world. And believing in God's magnificent power will make any disease disappear.

Faith Is the Most Essential Element in Healing Illness

At Happy Science, we practice a ritual prayer called, "El Cantare Healing."* This is a prayer for healing illnesses. This ritual prayer is only effective if the person offering it has faith in El Cantare. Without faith, the healing light will not flow in. But if we believe, we can become one with the soul of El Cantare, allowing His healing light to flow through us to reach and cure the sick.

We can perform this ritual prayer directly in front of the person who is sick. But this prayer is unique in that it can even heal someone who is physically away from the person offering it. Even if the person we are offering the prayer for is hundreds of miles away or even on the other side of the globe, the prayer can be as effective as if we were in the room with the person for whom we are performing the ritual.

The essential key to making this ritual prayer work is strong faith in the power of God. If those practicing the prayer firmly believe, from the bottom of their hearts, that God can both make the earth vanish and make it appear at His will, they will be endowed with the power to eliminate even cancer cells. Faith is the most important element in healing illnesses.

The New Testament tells stories of Jesus raising people from the dead. For example, when Jesus visited the man named Lazarus and cried out, "Lazarus, come out!" the dead man came back to life and came out of the tomb, still wrapped in cloth (John 11:43-44).

---

* This prayer is part of the "Prayer for Recovery from Illnesses" in one of the prayers books that are available only to Happy Science members.

Jesus brought dead men back to life. He helped the blind see and the physically disabled walk again. He transformed water into wine. He multiplied loaves and fishes and then fed a crowd of thousands. These events are not fictional stories but historical facts that actually took place. We can no longer perform these miracles today because people have lost the power of belief. Many Christian believers and theologians today don't really believe in the miracles that Jesus performed. They interpret these events as if they were parables or metaphors, because they do not understand the essence of miracle. They do not believe in the true power of God. When we believe, all things will be realized.

FAITH CAN SOLVE ANY PROBLEM

Staying Healthy Requires Commitment

Almost all the diseases that people today develop are caused by three factors: unbalanced diet, lack of exercise, and excessive stress. A combination of these unhealthy behaviors gives rise to most illnesses.

We can prevent diseases that have clear causes. In particular, we can avoid developing lifestyle diseases by starting to take preventive measures by our mid-thirties. Spoiling ourselves may cause costly damage to our health in the long run. If we continue to gorge on salty and high-calorie foods while neglecting exercise or constantly go to parties to drink, feast, and carouse, then it is only a matter of time before we get sick.

We need to watch our health not only for the sake of our own future, but also for the sake of our family. Taking care of our health is imperative if we want to continue to protect and support our family.

It takes effort and perseverance to avoid serious health risks. We need to commit ourselves to maintaining our health. We need to allocate considerable time for regular exercise and bear the drudgery of working out. When people say they don't have time for exercise, it's usually just an excuse. The real reason is often that they have given in to laziness or feel reluctant to try something new. I'm sure you can make time for exercise if you make up your mind to do so. Prioritizing your social life over your health is not a wise idea. Solitude is an essential part for your well-being.

You Can Cure Illness by Firmly Believing in Your Healing Power

Hospitals today are overly crowded with patients, but we should be aware that these medical facilities have often become nests of negative thoughts. Doctors tend to give pessimistic prognoses because they don't want to take the blame if a patient's condition gets worse than they had predicted. On the other hand, if the patient's condition improves, they can take credit for it. We should not give in to a negative prognosis, because this is the underlying reason for doctors' pessimistic view of our medical condition.

There is actually a lot we can do on our end to heal ourselves. Spiritual illness causes more than half of physical illnesses, so besides watching our diet and getting ample exercise, we can also improve our health by managing our state of mind.

So, we should not simply accept doctors' words at face value. Even if they told us that we have no chance of recovering, that we have only a year to live, or that we will be on medication for the rest of our life, we should take their prognosis with a grain of salt. We need to reject their negative thinking and tell ourselves firmly, "I am a child of God, so I have the power to heal myself," until we have convinced ourselves that we can cure ourselves of illness.

We are the architects of our own body. Whether consciously or unconsciously, our mind has built our body to be the way it is now. Our physical illness is the result of the negative thoughts and feelings we've had in our mind. When we consciously cultivate a strong desire to change our mind and hold onto that hope for recovery, we can change our physical condition.

Almost every illness is curable. Human beings have the potential to heal the diseases that are the leading causes of death, including cancer, heart disease, stroke, and vascular disease.

Of course, human beings are mortal, so death is inevitable in the end. But it is possible to avoid illness and death at crucial periods in our life, such as when we're in charge of an important project for our company or when no one else can provide for our family.

Faith and Effort Invite God's Healing Light

What opens up our path is our faith and persistent effort. First, we have to do what we can to break all unhealthy habits. Even God cannot save those who smoke packs of cigarettes every day and develop lung cancer as a result. Heaven can't help those who suffer from alcohol-induced liver disease because they drink a bottle of whisky every night.

If we really wish to cure a physical ailment, we need to strive to change the habits and behaviors that caused it. We have to come to a realization that we can't keep living the way we have been, and make up our mind to turn a new leaf. Continued efforts and faith are essential elements for recovering from illness. We can receive healing light and healing power that heaven pours on us if we have faith and make earnest efforts to improve our health.

To tell the truth, even heaven plays favorites, just as some schoolteachers show favoritism and offer extra help to good students. Becoming a good student in the eyes of God means living in a way that God cherishes, which means seeking a right mind and constantly striving to be pure of heart, loving, and kind.

Hatred and Anger Are Poisonous

In most cases, those who fall ill harbor feelings of hatred and anger within their heart. If you become sick, look within and see if you are holding any grudges. If you find a feeling of hatred toward anyone, that is most likely the cause of your ill-ness. So it is essential that you make peace with the person and stop bearing ill will toward him or her.

You may be laying all the blame on the other person, but that is probably not how he or she sees it, nor how God sees it. To you, this person may be an evil, hateful enemy who bullied and tortured you, but if these feelings are causing your illness, they are not worth holding onto.

Harboring hatred is detrimental to us. The grudge inside us keeps destroying our body, causing such diseases as cancer. We all know that it is silly to go poison ourselves. Hatred and anger are poisons of the mind, and harboring these feelings is the same as constantly taking poison.

If these feelings are causing your illness, however, it also means that you can cure yourself by letting go of them. The first step you can take is to practice self-reflection. Looking deep within and reflecting on your thoughts and feelings will improve your condition.

Religious Faith Gives You the Power to Completely Transform Yourself

If we keep on improving ourselves and become not just good student, but excellent student in the eyes of God, we may even be granted longer life. In fact, angels hold meetings to decide whether to extend someone's life. On most occasions, people have brought their disease on themselves, so there is nothing that even heaven can do about it. But if it is deemed necessary for someone to live longer so he or she can continue to contribute to the world, heaven grants the person longer life, and his or her illness is almost always cured.

In more than 90 percent of cases, those who fall ill have caused their illness themselves. Their own past thoughts and actions are the cause of illness, so it is difficult to sweep the slate completely clean. We get so accustomed to the tendencies and habits that we have built up over the years, that we cannot change them easily. It takes a lot of hard work to correct the course of our life.

Religious faith gives us the power to transcend the principles of this material world and enables us to regenerate and transform completely. It has the power to fundamentally change us. Through religious faith, we can not only cure diseases, but also remake ourselves.

I ask you never to give up hope, because no matter how difficult your circumstances are, you always have a chance to recover. You can always open up a new path. Even if one door closes, another one will open. Faith really is the power to solve everything. But faith also requires tireless effort on your part. Take in to heart, and never forget the importance of belief and devotion to the pursuit of your faith.

Hermes, the God of Medicine

The god Hermes was a hero who lived in Greece 4,300 years ago. He brought prosperity to the Mediterranean region and laid the foundations of Western civilization. Well-known as the god of commerce, prosperity, the arts, travel, and communications, Hermes is also known as the god of medicine. The wand of Hermes, known as the kerykeion or caduceus, is widely used around the world as a medical symbol.

Epilogue

MODERN MEDICINE AND RELIGION

Understanding the relationship between
Modern medical science and religion
Is a difficult challenge.

I believe that modern medicine
Is under Heaven's guidance.

The angels of light in the field of medical science,
Or the "medical gods," as we call them,
All have their spiritual roots in the god Hermes.

Eastern medicine sometimes takes opposing approaches to
The methods used in Western medicine.
Its principles have spiritual roots in Taoism and Buddhism,
As exemplified by the fact that
Medicine was often taught by monks and priests.

Divine spirits in heaven have been
Actively assisting and supporting
Religious practices for healing illnesses.
They have performed miracles,
From time to time,
To help people deepen their faith.

What is important is that medical science and religion
Cooperate and collaborate with each other.

Religious faith will enable physicians to use
The power of the mind to heal more illnesses.
It will also enable them, at times,
To use the combined power of
Positive words and medication to
Miraculously cure even the most deadly diseases.

Likewise, working with the positive aspects of
Medical science will allow religious practitioners to
Increase the number of souls they can save.

It is my hope that medical science and religion
Help each other achieve their shared goal of
Bringing happiness to people.

—*Ryuho Okawa, May 2008*

About the Author

RYUHO OKAWA is Global Visionary, renowned spiritual leader, and international best-selling author with a simple goal: to help people find true happiness and create a better world.

His deep compassion and sense of responsibility for the happiness of each individual has prompted him to publish over 2,200 titles of religious, spiritual, and self-development teachings, covering a broad range of topics including how our thoughts influence reality, the nature of love, and the path to enlightenment. He also writes on the topics of management and economy, as well as the relationship between religion and politics in the global context. To date, Okawa's books have sold over 100 million copies worldwide and been translated into 28 languages.

Okawa has dedicated himself to improving society and creating a better world. In 1986, Okawa founded Happy Science as a spiritual movement dedicated to bringing greater happiness to humankind by uniting religions and cultures to live in harmony. Happy Science has grown rapidly from its beginnings in Japan to a worldwide organization with over twelve million members. Okawa is compassionately committed to the spiritual growth of others. In addition to writing and publishing books, he continues to give lectures around the world.

About Happy Science

Happy Science is a global movement that empowers individuals to find purpose and spiritual happiness and to share that happiness with their families, societies, and the world. With more than twelve million members around the world, Happy Science aims to increase awareness of spiritual truths and expand our capacity for love, compassion, and joy so that together we can create the kind of world we all wish to live in.

Activities at Happy Science are based on the Principles of Happiness (Love, Wisdom, Self-Reflection, and Progress). These principles embrace worldwide philosophies and beliefs, transcending boundaries of culture and religions.

Love teaches us to give ourselves freely without expecting anything in return; it encompasses giving, nurturing, and forgiveness.

Wisdom leads us to the insights of spiritual truths, and opens us to the true meaning of life and the will of God (the universe, the highest power, Buddha).

Self-Reflection brings a mindful, nonjudgmental lens to our thoughts and actions to help us find our truest selves—the essence of our souls—and deepen our connection to the highest power. It helps us attain a clean and peaceful mind and leads us to the right life path.

Progress emphasizes the positive, dynamic aspects of our spiritual growth—actions we can take to manifest and spread happiness around the world. It's a path that not only expands our soul growth, but also furthers the collective potential of the world we live in.

Programs and Events

The doors of Happy Science are open to all. We offer a variety of programs and events, including self-exploration and self-growth programs, spiritual seminars, meditation and contemplation sessions, study groups, and book events.

Our programs are designed to:

- Deepen your understanding of your purpose and meaning in life
- Improve your relationships and increase your capacity to love unconditionally
- Attain a peace of mind, decrease anxiety and stress, and feel positive
- Gain deeper insights and broader perspective on the world
- Learn how to overcome life's challenges

    ... and much more.

For more information, visit happyscience-na.org or happy-science.org.

International Seminars

Each year, friends from all over the world join our international seminars, held at our faith centers in Japan. Different programs are offered each year and cover a wide variety of topics, including improving relationships, practicing the Eightfold Path to enlightenment, and loving yourself, to name just a few.

Happy Science Monthly

Our monthly publication covers the latest featured lectures, members' life-changing experiences and other news from members around the world, book reviews, and many other topics. Downloadable PDF files are available at happyscience-na.org. Copies and back issues in Portuguese, Chinese, and other languages are available upon request. For more information, contact us via e-mail at tokyo@happy-science.org.

Contact Information

Happy Science is a worldwide organization with faith centers around the globe. For a comprehensive list of centers, visit the worldwide directory at happy-science.org or happyscience-na.org. The following are some of the many Happy Science locations:

United States and Canada

New York
79 Franklin Street
New York, NY 10013
Phone: 212-343-7972
Fax: 212-343-7973
Email: ny@happy-science.org
Website: newyork.happyscience-na.org

San Francisco
525 Clinton Street
Redwood City, CA 94062
Phone&Fax: 650-363-2777
Email: sf@happy-science.org
Website: sanfrancisco.happyscience-na.org

Florida
5208 8th St.
Zephyrhills, FL 33542
Phone: 813-715-0000
Fax: 813-715-0010
Email: florida@happy-science.org
Website: florida.happyscience-na.org

New Jersey
725 River Rd. #102B
Edgewater, NJ 07020
Phone: 201-313-0127
Fax: 201-313-0120
Email: nj@happy-science.org
Website: newjersey.happyscience-na.org

Atlanta
1874 Piedmont Ave. NE
Suite 360-C
Atlanta, GA 30324
Phone: 404-892-7770
Email: atlanta@happy-science.org
Website: atlanta.happyscience-na.org

Los Angeles
1590 E. Del Mar Blvd.
Pasadena, CA 91106
Phone: 626-395-7775
Fax: 626-395-7776
Email: la@happy-science.org
Website: losangeles.happyscience-na.org

Orange County
10231 Slater Ave #204
Fountain Valley, CA 92708
Phone: 714-745-1140
Email: oc@happy-science.org

San Diego
7841 Balboa Ave.
Suite #202
San Diego, CA 92111
Phone: 619-381-7615
Fax: 626-395-7776
E-mail: sandiego@happy-science.org
Website: happyscience-la.org

Hawaii
1221 Kapiolani Blvd. Suite 920
Honolulu, HI 96814
Phone: 808-591-9772
Fax: 808-591-9776
Email: hi@happy-science.org
Website: hawaii.happyscience-na.org

Kauai
4504 Kukui Street
Dragon Building Suite 21
Kapaa, HI 96746
Phone: 808-822-7007
Fax: 808-822-6007
Email: kauai-hi@happy-science.org
Website: kauai.happyscience-na.org

Toronto
323 College Street
Toronto, ON M5T 1S2 Canada
Phone&Fax: 1-416-901-3747
Email: toronto@happy-science.org
Website: happy-science.ca

Vancouver
#212-2609 East 49th Avenue
Vancouver, BC,V5S 1J9 Canada
Phone: 1-604-437-7735
Fax: 1-604-437-7764
Email: vancouver@happy-science.org
Website: happy-science.ca

International

Tokyo
1-6-7 Togoshi, Shinagawa
Tokyo, 142-0041 Japan
Phone: 81-3-6384-5770
Fax: 81-3-6384-5776
Email: tokyo@happy-science.org
Website: happy-science.org

London
3 Margaret Street
London,W1W 8RE
United Kingdom
Phone: 44-20-7323-9255
Fax: 44-20-7323-9344
Email: eu@happy-science.org
Website: happyscience-uk.org

Sydney
516 Pacific Hwy Lane Cove North,
NSW 2066 Australia
Phone: 61-2-9411-2877
Fax: 61-2-9411-2822
Email: sydney@happy-science.org

Brazil Headquarters
Rua. Domingos de Morais 1154,
Vila Mariana, Sao Paulo,
SP-CEP 04009-002 Brazil
Phone: 55-11-5088-3800
Fax: 55-11-5088-3806
Email: sp@happy-science.org
Website: cienciadafelicidade.com.br

Jundiai
Rua Congo, 447, Jd. Bonfiglioli
Jundiai-CEP 13207-340
Phone: 55-11-4587-5952
Email: jundiai@happy-sciece.org

Seoul
74, Sadang-ro 27-gil,
Dongjak-gu, Seoul, Korea
Phone: 82-2-3478-8777
Fax: 82-2- 3478-9777
Email: korea@happy-science.org
Website: happyscience-korea.org

Taipei
No. 89, Lane 155, Dunhua N. Road
Songshan District,
Taipei City, 105 Taiwan
Phone: 886-2-2719-9377
Fax: 886-2-2719-5570
Email: taiwan@happy-science.org
Website: happyscience-tw.org

Malaysia
No 22A, Block2, Jalil Link Jalan
Jalil Jaya 2, Bukit Jalil 57000
Kuala Lumpur, Malaysia
Phone: 60-3-8998-7877
Fax: 60-3-8998-7977
Email: malaysia@happy-science.org
Website: happyscience.org.my

Nepal
Kathmandu Metropolitan City
Ward No. 15, Ring Road,
Kimdol, Sitapaila
Kathmandu, Nepal
Phone: 97-714-272931
Email: nepal@happy-science.org

Uganda
Plot 877 Rubaga Road
Kampala P.O. Box 34130
Kampala, Uganda
Phone: 256-79-3238-002
Email: uganda@happy-science.org
Website: happyscience-uganda.org

About IRH Press USA Inc.

IRH Press USA Inc. was founded in 2013 as an affiliated firm of IRH Press Co., Ltd. Based in New York, the press publishes books in various categories including spirituality, religion, and self-improvement and publishes books by Ryuho Okawa, the author of 100 million books sold worldwide. For more information, visit OkawaBooks.com.

Follow us on:

Facebook: MasterOkawaBooks

Twitter: OkawaBooks

Goodreads: RyuhoOkawa

Instagram: OkawaBooks

Pinterest: OkawaBooks

Books by Ryuho Okawa

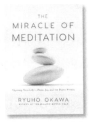

THE MIRACLE OF MEDITATION
Opening Your Life to Peace, Joy, and the Power Within

Softcover ⬩ 208 pages ⬩ $15.95 ⬩ ISBN: 978-1-942125-09-9

Meditation can open your mind to the self-transformative potential within and connect your soul to the wisdom of heaven—all through the power of belief. This book combines the power of faith and the practice of meditation to help you create inner peace, discover your inner divinity, become your ideal self, and cultivate a purposeful life of altruism and compassion.

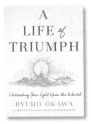

A LIFE OF TRIUMPH
Unleashing Your Light Upon the World

Softcover ⬩ 240 pages ⬩ $15.95 ⬩ ISBN: 978-1-942125-11-2

There is a power within you that can lift your heart from despair to hope, from hardship to happiness, and from defeat to triumph. In this book, Ryuho Okawa explains the key attitudes that will help you continuously tap the everlasting reserves of positivity, courage, and energy that are already a part of you so you can realize your dreams and become a wellspring of happiness. You'll also find many inspirational poems and a contemplation exercise to inspirit your inner light in times of adversity and in your day-to-day life.

THE UNHAPPINESS SYNDROME
28 Habits of Unhappy People (and How to Change Them)

THE LAWS OF SUCCESS
A Spiritual Guide to Turning Your Hopes into Reality

THE ESSENCE OF BUDDHA
The Path to Enlightenment

THE LAWS OF JUSTICE
How We Can Solve World Conflicts and Bring Peace

THE HEART OF WORK
10 Keys to Living Your Calling

THINK BIG!
Be Positive and Be Brave to Achieve Your Dreams

INVITATION TO HAPPINESS
7 Inspirations from Your Inner Angel

MESSAGES FROM HEAVEN
What Jesus, Buddha, Muhammad, and Moses Would Say Today

THE LAWS OF THE SUN
One Source, One Planet, One People

SECRETS OF THE EVERLASTING TRUTHS
A New Paradigm for Living on Earth

THE NINE DIMENSIONS
Unveiling the Laws of Eternity

THE MOMENT OF TRUTH
Become a Living Angel Today

CHANGE YOUR LIFE, CHANGE THE WORLD
A Spiritual Guide to Living Now

For a complete list of books, visit OkawaBooks.com.